Inexpressible
Island

Mt Baxter

N

Priestley Glacier

Mt Nansen

Fossil Wood Moraine

Nansen Foothills

C. Sastrugi

Creva

Reeves
Glacier

Reeves Nunatak

Vegetatio

Inexpressibl

Mt Larsen

Inlet 170 paces broad

DR

Nat. Scale 1: 500,000 or 1 Inch.= 7.89 Stat. Miles.

10   5   0   10 Mls.

Routes   ⟶

evick

Inexpressible Island

Heavy
Icefalls — Mt Melbourne

Mt Dickason

Boomerang Gl.

Campbell Glacier

Mt Browning

hony Pt.

Mt Abbott
(2860 approx.)

T E R R A

Hells Gate (Depot Moraine Camp)
Lat. 74° 56' S.
Northern
Foothills

vans Coves

N O V A

B A Y

EVANS COVES DISTRICT
(The Cross marks the position of the
snowdrift on which the Northern Party lived.)

KI

UE

Inexpressible Island
first published 1998 by
Scirocco Drama
An imprint of J. Gordon Shillingford Publishing Inc.
© 1997 David Young

Scirocco Drama Editor: Dave Carley
Cover design by Bob Wilcox and Terry Gallagher/Doowah Design
Author Photo by V. Tony Hauser
Printed and bound in Canada

This play is a work of fiction inspired by real events that took place in Antarctica in 1912.

We acknowledge the support of The Canada Council for the Arts and
the Manitoba Arts Council for our publishing program.

Canadian Cataloguing in Publication Data

Young, David, 1946–
        Inexpressible Island
    A play.
    ISBN 1-896239-31-5
        I. Title.
PS8597.O59I54 1998   C812'.54   C98-900367-1
PR9199.3.Y58I55 1998

Production Credits

Inexpressible Island, produced by Necessary Angel Theatre Company, premiered at Canadian Stage Theatre, Toronto, on September 18, 1997 with the following cast:

CAMPBELL .... R.H. Thomson
LEVICK .... Richard McMillan
PRIESTLEY .... Graham Harley
DICKASON .... Victor Ertmanis
BROWNING .... Julian Richings
ABBOTT .... Wayne Best

Directed by Richard Rose
Set and Light Design by Graeme S. Thomson
Constume Design by Charlotte Dean
Stage Manager: Susan Monis
Wardrobe: Sylvia Defend, Avril Stevenson, MaryJo Carter
Music Consultant: Don Horsburgh
Soundscape: Todd Charlton
Prop Consultant: Lisa Nighswander

Music: Northern Lights 1, Chinook, Chinook Whispers, Hocket.

All compositions Copyright Meredith Monk (ASCAP). Available on the *Facing North* album, ©1992 ECM Records.

David Young

David Young's last play, *Glenn*, was nominated for seven Dora Mavor Moore awards, the Chalmers Award and the Governor General's Award. His other plays (with Paul LeDoux) include *Fire* (Chalmers Award, four Dora awards) and *Love is Strange*. David has also written extensively for radio, film and television and is the author of two novels. He was the President of Coach House Press for ten years.

Playwright's Notes

This play is a work of fiction based on real events that took place in Antarctica in 1912. It follows feeling rather than historical scholarship.

While Captain Scott was making his ill-fated attempt on the South Pole, a scientific party attached to his expedition was surveying another region of the continent. In its day, this kind of expedition was the equivalent of a voyage to the moon.

Scott and his party perished on or about March 29, 1912. Their bodies were discovered in the tent (with Scott's famous final letters) nearly eight months later. This eight month hiatus neatly brackets the period during which the scientific party lead by Lieutenant Campbell underwent the ordeal dramatized in this play. Their safe return to Hut Point was completely eclipsed by Scott's tragedy. Today their achievement has been all but forgotten.

The play is dedicated to the memory of these men and to my mother Toto, the best of the English.

The Northern Party at Cape Adare.
Left to right, standing, Abbot, Dickason, Browning.
Left to right, seated, Priestley, Campbell, Levick.

Cast

The Officers

LIEUTENANT CAMPBELL (aka Number One), 35, Royal Navy officer in command of the expedition

DR. LEVICK (aka Mother), 32, Royal Navy, the expedition's medical officer, second-in-command

PRIESTLEY (aka Mr. Nipcheese), 29, a civilian geologist attached to the expedition

The Men

DICKASON (aka Dog), 30, signalman, an enlisted man in the Royal Navy

BROWNING (aka Rings), 29, a Royal Navy seaman

ABBOTT (aka Tiny), 28, a stoker in the Royal Navy

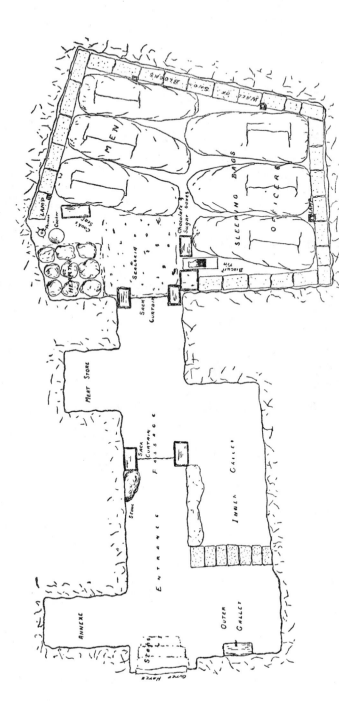

PLAN OF IGLOO.

"What catches and holds the imagination of the English is not successful achievement in the ordinary sense. What they cherish, even though most would immediately deny it, is any action, though it may be accounted a failure, that appears when it is recorded to be epic, that takes on a poetic quality, that haunts the mind like myth."
    —J.B. Priestly, *The Edwardians*

"The true religious force in the world is not the church but the world itself."
    —Wallace Stevens

ACT ONE

(Music under: From "Pomp and Circumstance".

Light fades.

Music cross-fades to: Meredith Monk.

*The dim half-light of an Antarctic autumn. Every-
thing is white, the shadows lime green and mauve
and madder rose. Every volume steamlined by aeons
of wind. The overall effect is both spare and complex.*

*The back of the playing area is defined by a great
wind-sculpted surface, undulating waves and
ridges of ice that create a painterly interplay of light
and shadow. A smooth-walled opening in this surface functions as an entry/exit and vanishing point.*

A chair and side table are set near the apron.

*The lights dim, the scene glows violet, amber and
rose: the hues of Antarctic twilight.*

Sound: a wind.

*As the light fades the wind builds in intensity, from
moderate gale, to whole gale, and full storm.*

*Five men enter the half-light, moving in slow
motion, fighting the storm together. One of their
number is in desperate condition. The other four
drop to hands and knees, clinging to him as they
battle the ferocious wind and seek to erect what
remains of a tent canvas. A scene of terrible
suffering.*

Sound: wind subsides.

Light shift: To favour PRIESTLEY, dozing in his chair. He startles awake.)

PRIESTLEY: Best days of my life...that wind, month upon month, it scoured us clean. Clarity. Intensity.

(He opens a tattered journal with trembling hands and begins to read.)

March 1st, 1912. Ten degrees of frost with a full gale blowing round the clock. The *Terra Nova* is now a week overdue. We have been without proper shelter since our only remaining tent was damaged in a storm. One might survive an Antarctic winter with proper clothing and rations but after three months of summer sledging our supplies are down to a nub.

Less than a pint of fuel left for the primus stove. No proper winter garments. Our reindeer bags sodden. We sit in them and chew raw seal blubber, waiting for the *Terra Nova* to relieve us and end this nightmare.

(PRIESTLEY closes the journal. Closes his eyes, remembering.)

(Singing.) To be a pilgrim...

(SFX: a Weddell Seal.

Light shift. There is movement under the tent canvas.)

CAMPBELL: *(Off.)* Dinner bell, get a move on. Rise and shine. Rise and shine. The day is fine. Show a leg, show a leg. Dickason, may we have a report, please?

(DICKASON appears from beneath the tarp, looks around.)

DICKASON: *(To himself.)* Not dressed for this.

(He comes to his feet. He's in ragged summer sledging gear. CAMPBELL clambers out of his sleeping bag, does a little warm-up dance, and moves to stand with DICKASON.)

Fuzzy nothingness, sir.

CAMPBELL: *(Pointing, impatient.)* Ice blink.

DICKASON: As you say, sir.

> *(Sound: Weddell Seal.)*

CAMPBELL: Fetch the killing stave.

DICKASON: Aye-aye, sir.

> *(DICKASON re-enters the tent to retrieve a stout club with a metal hook on one end from under the tent canvas.*
>
> *CAMPBELL moves to a fully-loaded manhauling sledge. He tries to loosen off a knot. The cold hurts his hands. He pulls a coiled rope clear of the sledge, frustrated.)*

CAMPBELL: Can't manage the knot. Fetch us some tea.

> *(Sound: Weddell Seal.)*

Dr. Levick—

LEVICK: *(Off.)* Yes, sir.

> *(LEVICK's head appears from the tent.)*

CAMPBELL: Browning's status, please.

LEVICK: A moment, sir.

> *(LEVICK disappears from view. CAMPBELL watches DICKASON untie the knot. His hands are bare.)*

CAMPBELL: Don't know how you do it, Dickie.

DICKASON: A place for everything and everything in its place, sir.

CAMPBELL: Your hands.

> *(DICKASON passes CAMPBELL the tea bags.)*

DICKASON: I'm growing claws, sir.

(LEVICK reappears, comes to his feet.)

LEVICK: Badly dehydrated, I'm afraid.

CAMPBELL: *(Handing tea bags.)* Brew him some tea with extra sugar. Give him *a quarter* of a biscuit.

LEVICK: Yes sir.

DICKASON: The day bag seems to have gone missing, sir.

CAMPBELL: Impossible.

DICKASON: I lashed it right here.

CAMPBELL: Well, it must be there!

DICKASON: It was blowing a hurricane when I stowed it, sir.

(CAMPBELL is furious. He covers it.)

CAMPBELL: Resecure the sledge. We'll sort it out later. We've got our work cut out for us here, Dr. Levick. No one is feeling particularly fit. We're about to lose the light. You understand my concern?

LEVICK: Completely, sir.

CAMPBELL: I have no wish to further weaken the man.

LEVICK: I'll see what I can do.

(Sound: Weddell Seal.

LEVICK disappears from view.)

CAMPBELL: Mr. Priestley—

(PRIESTLEY's eyes pop open, he sits up in his chair. Amazed and atremble.)

PRIESTLEY: Sir?

CAMPBELL: *(Approaching.)* We've got a male close by.

PRIESTLEY: Ready when you are.

(PRIESTLEY tries to still his trembling hand.)

CAMPBELL: We must build a weather wall for the food cache.

PRIESTLEY: Absolutely vital.

CAMPBELL: Did you hear that, Abbott?

ABBOTT: *(Off.)* Yes, sir.

CAMPBELL: Room for eighty penguin and fifty seal.

> *(ABBOTT's head appears.)*

ABBOTT: *(Horror.)* We're staying?

> *(Sound: wind burst.*
>
> *They huddle away from the blast.*
>
> *Sound: wind subsides.*
>
> *CAMPBELL passes the rope to DICKASON. DICKASON ties in. ABBOTT pulls on his boots, not pleased.)*

CAMPBELL: *(Concern.)* Mr. Priestley—

> *(PRIESTLEY turns to face CAMPBELL for the first time. His tremble vanishes.)*

PRIESTLEY: Sir?

CAMPBELL: Are you with us?

PRIESTLEY: Just daydreaming, sir.

> *(CAMPBELL moves to take PRIESTLEY into his confidence.)*

CAMPBELL: We've had a bit of a disaster with the day bag.

PRIESTLEY: Oh dear.

CAMPBELL: A week's food. Probably halfway to New Zealand by now.

PRIESTLEY: My-my-my.

CAMPBELL: *(Meaning the weather.)* It could thicken up on us.

PRIESTLEY: No surprise there.

> *(Sound: Weddell Seal.)*

CAMPBELL: *(To DICKASON,)* Mr. Priestley will accompany us.

                (DICKASON throws PRIESTLEY the rope. PRIESTLEY ties in.)

DICKASON: Sir, I am so sorry.

CAMPBELL: Nothing to be done.

DICKASON: We need all we got, sir.

CAMPBELL: Indeed we do. Follow on.

                (CAMPBELL leads DICKASON off. PRIESTLEY is pulled into the scene, still wearing his shirt and tie. The group disappears behind an ice formation.

                LEVICK comes to his feet, does his warm-up dance.)

LEVICK: Come along, Tiny. Show a leg.

                ('Tiny' ABBOTT comes to his feet.)

ABBOTT: Don't fancy another night in that bog.

LEVICK: We may be able to jerry-rig some new bamboos.

ABBOTT: The crown piece is in ribbons!

LEVICK: Perhaps we can repair it.

ABBOTT: Perhaps we can walk on water.

LEVICK: Excuse me?

ABBOTT: Nothing, sir.

LEVICK: I don't like your tone of voice, Abbott.

                (LEVICK gives ABBOTT a look. ABBOTT nudges a reindeer skin sleeping bag with his toe.)

ABBOTT: Maybe we should give that make and mend to our friend Rings. Repair the tent! *(Shakes bag.)* What's that? I can't hear you, Browning.

                (BROWNING groans from inside his bag. LEVICK is fed up with ABBOTT's behaviour.)

LEVICK: Try and move around a little, Rings.

               *(BROWNING drags himself clear of his bag, stays
               down on all fours, groaning. His whole body is chat-
               tering.)*

BROWNING: I'm knackered, sir.

LEVICK: The raw seal. Your system is still adjusting.

ABBOTT: Karachi tooters. The man runs like a bleeding tap.

               (BROWNING stands, a slight man.)

BROWNING: I shall be just fine.

LEVICK: That's the ticket.

               (Sound: wind burst.

               *The men huddle away from the blast. BROWNING
               drops down on all fours and buries his head in his
               arms. He howls in pain. ABBOTT crawls to comfort
               him as the wind subsides.)*

ABBOTT: We'll be out of this soon enough, Rings.

BROWNING: You think so?

ABBOTT: *(Mad cackle.)* I'm not spending the bleeding winter
               here.

BROWNING: Six months in a pitch black hurricane. I—I don't
               think I'd manage.

LEVICK: *(Out of patience.)* Abbott, Lieutenant Campbell or-
               dered you to secure the larder.

ABBOTT: On the double, sir.

               *(ABBOTT ambles off. LEVICK looks BROWNING
               in the eye.)*

LEVICK: How are we going, Rings?

BROWNING: I'm afraid I had a bit of an accident in the night,
               Mother.

LEVICK: I have some spares. Not exactly clean, mind you.

BROWNING: Keep those for your own, sir.

LEVICK: Nonsense.

               (LEVICK moves to retrieve gear from his sleeping bag. BROWNING struggles for warmth.)

BROWNING: Are we going home, sir?

               (The question brings LEVICK up short.)

LEVICK: I have no idea.

BROWNING: I must know, sir.

LEVICK: I can't help you there.

BROWNING: But sir, another night like this, I don't think I can—

LEVICK: None of it, Browning! *(Gentle.)* You have a gippy tummy. It makes things seem far worse than they are.

               (BROWNING clutches his stomach, fighting a cramp.)

LEVICK: Empty yourself if you can. I'll fetch you some bismuth.

               (They exit.

               Sound: Weddell Seal.

               Light shift.

               CAMPBELL trudges on, leaning into the wind, secured by rope to DICKASON and PRIESTLEY. PRIESTLEY is in ragged summer sledging gear now. CAMPBELL applies his telescope to the horizon.)

DICKASON: Come on, Mr. Weddell, come on.

               (Sound: Weddell Seal.)

CAMPBELL: He's taunting us.

PRIESTLEY: Difficult seeing, sir.

CAMPBELL: A blank page.

(CAMPBELL lowers his telescope.)

Bugger be damned. We need a seal. Mr. Priestley, a word…

(PRIESTLEY and CAMPBELL move together. The rope attaching them to DICKASON stretches taut. DICKASON adjusts; he knows he's not meant to hear the conversation.)

You're not Royal Navy, Priestley, a steady hand nonetheless.

PRIESTLEY: I do my best, sir.

CAMPBELL: From now on you are in charge of stores. We've lost a day bag. Men are dipping into rations, carting food around loose in their pockets. You must bring some rigour to the situation. Gunroom discipline, Mr. Priestley.

PRIESTLEY: Might Dr. Levick not feel that I'm encroaching on his territory, sir? He has a pretty thorough understanding of nutrition.

(CAMPBELL rubs at frostbite on PRIESTLEY's cheek.)

CAMPBELL: I don't think Dr. Levick has entirely grasped our situation. He distributed chocolate yesterday as if we had an infinite supply.

PRIESTLEY: .He was trying to lift the men's spirits.

CAMPBELL: One doesn't achieve that by distributing stores we shall need in four months time. The men would finish off our rations in a week if we let them. I want a rationing blueprint for seven months.

PRIESTLEY: Is it beyond hope, sir?

(Sound: Weddell Seal.)

DICKASON: Sir! There! *(Pointing.)* A black speck!

CAMPBELL: *(To DICKASON.)* On him!

(They exit. BROWNING scuttles on, moving in a low stoop. Pants half off.)

BROWNING: *(Pointing.)* The ship. The ship!

(ABBOTT enters and moves to join BROWNING.)

LEVICK: Where?

BROWNING: There! A black speck! Out past the Drygalski!

LEVICK: I don't see it.

BROWNING: A smudge of smoke.

ABBOTT: Yeah…I think I see that. There! Yes! There!

(They shout and wave.)

BROWNING: She must be running for cover.

(LEVICK has applied his monocular to the horizon.)

LEVICK: There's no ship. *(To BROWNING.)* Back in your bag.

CAMPBELL: *(Off, distant.)* Tea-oh!

(LEVICK wheels and looks toward the vanishing point with his monocular.)

LEVICK: Jolly good! They've bagged one!

(LEVICK and ABBOTT exit.

Alone now, BROWNING leans into his sledging harness which is attached to a rope anchored through the vanishing point.)

BROWNING: You can never trust your eyes in the south. *(Marching in place.)* Out sledging on the barrier, I spied a hut in the distance. Men moving about, a curl of steam from the primus, laughter at half a mile, the yelp of their dogs.

A few minutes later I discovered the hut I'd been pulling toward was, in fact, an empty biscuit tin that'd come off the back of Dickason's sledge. Such is the intensity of the light here. The clarity of the air. You plod along, staring straight down at the snow as the day passes…inch by inch…a little thought will appear in the corner of your mind and grow and grow until it fills the entire sky. I remember an endless discussion about cold snaps. Was this the normal condition of the barrier or was it a cold snap? How cold did cold have to be in the Antarctic to qualify as a cold snap? The discussion lasted about a week.

…suddenly, the sound of your footsteps shifts—a soft *creesh*—a moment later, *booomph!*

(He falls, hanging head first toward the audience.)

Walls of blue ice dropping straight away into the black of nowhere. You're hung in your harness down the throat of a crevasse. The strange silence of it all. Upside down. The ice surface an inch from your eye. Little bubbles of air trapped there. One day up on the Beardmore Glacier I broke through eight times.

(LEVICK and ABBOTT appear in tableau in the vanishing point, as if leaning over the edge of a crevasse.)

The last time a whole string of dogs went through with me. I was hung down there among 'em, the lot of us suspended over eternity, and they started fighting in their traces. Snapping and snarling and tearing each other to bits…right inside my head. *(Pause.)* Eighteen months in the south. The riches of the place have begun to wear on me.

(BROWNING regains his feet.)

I won't survive a winter here. I can't hold the seal meat down…and we have nothing else. *(Pause.)* The little toe on my left foot has gone black. I've not told a soul.

(Sound: giant wind burst.

Light: snap to black.

          The men's voices are carried off by the wind as they
          fight the storm.)

CAMPBELL: *(Off.)* Dr. Levick!

LEVICK: *(Off.)* Here!

CAMPBELL: *(Off.)* Mr. Priestley! *(Pause.)* Mr. Priestley!

PRIESTLEY: *(Off.)* Here!

CAMPBELL: *(Off.)* Dickason!

DICKASON: *(Off.)* Sir!

CAMPBELL: *(Off.)* Abbott!

ABBOTT: *(Off.)* Here!

CAMPBELL: *(Off.)* Browning? *(Pause, sharp.)* Dr. Levick?

          (Sound: storm abates.

          Lights up.)

LEVICK: He's been moving, sir.

CAMPBELL: Then he should respond.

BROWNING: *(Off, weak.)* Sir.

          (The party slept like a ball of hibernating snakes.
          CAMPBELL is on his feet in a hypothermic stupor.
          He moves to warm himself, a crazed dance, panic
          brimming up. He checks the empty horizon.)

CAMPBELL: *(To himself.)* Bloody hell.

          (CAMPBELL regains control and moves back to the
          pile of sleeping bags.)

          On your feet! Up-up-up-up-up! Horrendous night,
          gentlemen. We must do better.

BROWNING: *(Head appears.)* Ship?

CAMPBELL: Brash ice all the way out. Nothing.

          (CAMPBELL looks from man to man, beaming as if
          this is wonderful news.)

BROWNING: Doom.

CAMPBELL: Gentlemen, it is official. We shall be overwintering on this shore.

(*BROWNING groans.*)

LEVICK: How are the cramps?

BROWNING: Bad, sir.

CAMPBELL: On your feet, Browning.

(*ABBOTT and LEVICK help BROWNING to his feet, rub him vigorously.*)

CAMPBELL: Tight corner, Browning, we have our training! We follow in the footsteps of Drake, Raleigh and Cook. Glory in adversity. Splendour in misfortune. A harvest of joy raised upon a battlefield of suffering! We will draw a circle round ourselves. We will pull as one. We will survive!

PRIESTLEY: At your command, sir!

CAMPBELL: Smartly done, Priestley.

LEVICK: We'll make a Bluejacket of him yet.

ABBOTT: That'll be the day.

BROWNING: All winter, sir?

(*BROWNING's face collapses, a silent howl.*)

CAMPBELL: Browning—

BROWNING: I cannot help myself, sir.

CAMPBELL: You can! You must!

BROWNING: Sir, I am simply worried that—

CAMPBELL: (*Interrupting.*) We are all worried. The energy we use worrying could be put to better use. You understand my meaning, Browning?

BROWNING: I do, sir.

CAMPBELL: Very well then. I have been thinking. I have a plan. These are my new orders. We will stick with the two team approach. Dr. Levick, Abbott and Browning will work to enlarge the cave. I have put Mr. Priestley in charge of stores.

(LEVICK is stung. He smiles gamely.)

LEVICK: Jolly good.

CAMPBELL: *(To PRIESTLEY.)* Reduced rations until we are safe in our shelter. Biscuit ration cut by half. Sugar, chocolate and raisins cut out altogether. No exceptions! *(To LEVICK.)* The front part of the drift is unstable. You must dig further back into it before enlarging the sleeping chamber. *(To DICKASON.)* You and Mr. Priestley will patrol the ice front between here and Hell's Gate. *(To PRIESTLEY.)* How many animals do we have?

PRIESTLEY: Eighteen penguin and fifteen seal.

CAMPBELL: Penguins are moving north. We'll need at least fifty more seals to see us through.

LEVICK: I would have thought forty.

CAMPBELL: We have refined all our calculations, Dr. Levick.

LEVICK: I see. Jolly good.

CAMPBELL: Gentlemen, our way is clear.

(CAMPBELL picks up a block of snow and begins to sing. The men join him in the work and the plainsong as they set about building the cave.

Light shift: to lower levels.)

We praise Thee, O God.

MEN: We praise Thee, O God.

CAMPBELL: We acknowledge Thee to be the Lord.

MEN: We acknowledge Thee to be the Lord.

CAMPBELL: All the earth doth worship Thee.

MEN: All the earth doth worship Thee.

CAMPBELL: The Father everlasting.

MEN: The Father everlasting.

(Focus on BROWNING, his growing torment.)

ALL: To Thee all Angels/ Cry aloud: The Heavens and all the powers therein, To Thee / Cherubim and Seraphim continually do cry / Holy Holy Holy: Lord God of Saba-oth / Heaven and Earth are full of the Majesty of Thy glory / The glorious company of the Apostles: praise Thee / The goodly fellowship of the Prophets: praise Thee.

(The party gets into their reindeer skin bags. BROWNING loses control entirely and sobs like a baby.)

BROWNING: Seven months. Seven months. Seven months.

CAMPBELL: *(Quietly, to DICKASON.)* Fetch my hymnal from the sledge.

(BROWNING falls into PRIESTLEY's arms. PRIESTLEY is out of his depth; BROWNING's despair terrifies him. ABBOTT moves to comfort BROWNING.)

ABBOTT: *(Whisper, to PRIESTLEY.)* You don't belong here, do you?

(The fierce energy in ABBOTT's eyes drives PRIESTLEY from the shelter. DICKASON stumbles from the cave.)

DICKASON: *(Awe.)* My-my. What a lot of books.

(Light shift: to imply firelight downstage.

PRIESTLEY moves to join DICKASON. His Parkinson tremble returns.)

PRIESTLEY: I'm not sure if I keep them or they keep me, Dickason. *(Pause.)* Thank you for coming.

DICKASON: It was an honour to be included, sir.

PRIESTLEY: A small memorial service. Just the two of us and
              the immediate family. Mrs. Levick felt we be-
              longed…

DICKASON: Did he have children, sir?

PRIESTLEY: A son who predeceased him.

DICKASON: Such a man—

PRIESTLEY: She wants me to say a few words. I've been reread-
              ing my journals, looking for an appropriate pas-
              sage. No luck.

              (He tosses his journal in the chair.)

              Not a mention of our overwintering in the *Times*
              obituary. *(Laugh.)* Perhaps we never went south.
              Perhaps I imagined the whole thing.

              *(DICKASON laughs a little too loud, still not
              gauging the flow of things.)*

              We'll be forgotten, Dickie. That's our fate.

DICKASON: It's Captain Scott they want to remember, sir.

PRIESTLEY: *(Disgust.)* Starving in his tent…*(Pause.)* Well. Here
              we are. So.

              *(It's been a long time. These two are total stran-
              gers.)*

DICKASON: I hear of your honours, Sir Raymond.

PRIESTLEY: Cambridge has been a kind of home.

DICKASON: And your writings, I've not read the books, sir, but
              I know of them.

PRIESTLEY: A mere popularizer. I sow the seeds of other men's
              science.

DICKASON: Have you written about our time in the south, sir?

PRIESTLEY: Sketching personalities was never my strong suit.
              I'm attuned to the testimony of things, Dickie. *Old*
              rocks. Six hundred million years ago such and so

happened. Human history? Much too recent to be of any consequence! *(Smile.)* The closer I get to the place where I stand, the less I know about it.

DICKASON: You could publish your journal, sir.

PRIESTLEY: Nothing there! Wall to wall decorum. I was too young, too caught up in the system, I couldn't see. *(Pause.)* I *can't* see…we went into the black, Dickie. We left this world behind.

DICKASON: Title's easy, sir. 'Six Men in an Icy Tomb'.

PRIESTLEY: *(Taps temple.)* This is the tomb, Dickie. Tick. Tick. Tick. Time runs on…

> *(Pause. PRIESTLEY stares off into space, uncomfortable with his thoughts. DICKASON is aware of his physical frailty.)*

Never mind all that. Where are you these days?

DICKASON: Been mating on a pilot's tender out of Mousehole, sir. Coastal traders, mostly.

PRIESTLEY: Sounds pretty soft.

DICKASON: Cushy it is, and well deserved. I've faced my last lion, guv.

PRIESTLEY: You look in the pink.

DICKASON: You as well, sir.

PRIESTLEY: Residual nerve damage. Doing my best, under the circumstances.

DICKASON: I've got the gallstones, of course. We've all got'em, I imagine.

PRIESTLEY: That accursed diet—

DICKASON: Salt water in the hoosh.

PRIESTLEY: Eyeballs!

DICKASON: I never ate an eyeball, sir.

PRIESTLEY: Oh now—

DICKASON: *(Laughing.)* A filthy lie!

PRIESTLEY: Did you actually eat Browning's socks? Or did I make that up?

DICKASON: A man does as he must.

              (They share a laugh, it dwindles away. An uncomfortable pause.)

              Funny, what one remembers...

PRIESTLEY: I remember Abbott. He was the key, wasn't he?

DICKASON: What do you mean, sir?

PRIESTLEY: He saved us. That's what I think. If he'd been with the Pole party he'd have saved Scott.

DICKASON: How?

PRIESTLEY: Torn at him with his teeth. Driven him from the tent. *(Doing ABBOTT.)* You'll not die in your bag, you swanky bastard! Up and into it!

              (DICKASON laughs.)

DICKASON: *(Serious.)* A murderer's heart, sir, let's not forget that.

PRIESTLEY: Hm. The lizard's tail.

DICKASON: Sir?

PRIESTLEY: The lizard's tail. Browning's dream.

DICKASON: I—I'm sorry, sir. I don't know what you're talking about.

              (Pause.)

PRIESTLEY: What do you remember?

DICKASON: An endless night. Cold. Windy. *(Pause.)* Most of all, the peace.

PRIESTLEY: *(Laugh.)* It never stopped howling.

DICKASON: Lying in our bags thinking about the next biscuit...

PRIESTLEY: Such vast expanses of time. *(Pause.)* They rolled the day forward like a great boulder.

DICKASON: The pyramids! The lectures!

                (Their laughter peaks and subsides they step back towards the cave.)

PRIESTLEY: Dear Dr. Levick…

DICKASON: After all he'd been through, to drop dead during a waltz at a charity ball…

PRIESTLEY: I'll pour us a sherry. We'll light candles. One for each of us still living.

DICKASON: That would be fitting, sir.

                (They sit in the cave.)

PRIESTLEY: Two gone in the same year. It's passing strange.

DICKASON: It's the two who gorged in their dreams, sir. Did you ever think of that?

PRIESTLEY: No, Dickason, I didn't.

                (They settle into their bags. PRIESTLEY prepares to strike a match with shaking hand.

                Lights snap to black.

                Sound: wind. A distant moan.

                Sound: match being struck. Once. Twice.)

PRIESTLEY: *(Off.)* My fingers are shattered.

CAMPBELL: *(Off.)* Give it over to Dickason. He's got the surer hand in these matters.

PRIESTLEY: *(Off.)* As you say, sir.

BROWNING: *(Off.)* Make us all happy, Dog.

                (The match lights, revealing the snow cave.

                The reindeer sleeping bags are laid out three to a side. ABBOTT lies in the far corner, opposite

CAMPBELL. BROWNING is in the middle, opposite LEVICK. DICKASON is opposite PRIESTLEY.

DICKASON holds his match to an Oxo tin lamp held by BROWNING. The wick lights. An audible sigh of relief.)

DICKASON: Look at that, will you. Just look at that.

CAMPBELL: Bravo, Browning.

LEVICK: You're in glory, boy.

BROWNING: Strand of wick, safety pin, Oxo tin—Bob's your uncle.

(DICKASON lights other lamps.)

LEVICK: Isn't the flame wonderful?

PRIESTLEY: I'm feeling warm already.

CAMPBELL: Gentlemen, it is official, we are home.

(ABBOTT runs his hand around the curve of the ceiling.)

ABBOTT: Tight as a bull's arse.

CAMPBELL: From this point onwards Dickason and Dickason alone will handle matches. We have sufficient but we must be cautious. Smokers will use the lamps to light up after mess.

ABBOTT: Right, then—

(ABBOTT lights his fag. Smokes.)

CAMPBELL: Mr. Priestley, if you could highlight the situation vis-à-vis rations.

PRIESTLEY: I have apportioned half of our available supplies over the next seven months. The rest of our provisions will be held in reserve for the overland journey back to Hut Point. It breaks down as follows: Twelve cubes of sugar on Sunday. One-and-one-half ounces of chocolate every Saturday and alternate Wednesdays. Twenty-five muscatel raisins on the last day of each month. This division leaves a small margin for birthdays, of which there will be three between now and the end of the darkness.

LEVICK: Jolly good.

DICKASON: *(To himself.)* Twelve cubes Sunday. One and one half ounces Saturday...alternate Wednesdays.

BROWNING: Twenty-five muscatel raisins at the end of each month.

ABBOTT: *(A curse.)* For seven months.

CAMPBELL: So be it.

> *(Pause. ABBOTT picks up his empty bowl and spoon. Scrapes at the bowl. Tink-a-tink-a-tink.)*

ABBOTT: What about biscuits?

PRIESTLEY: We'll stay at one per day. I have opened a fresh tin.

> *(PRIESTLEY produces the tin. All eyes are on him. He opens it.)*

BROWNING: Badly broken, sir?

PRIESTLEY: Smashed to smithereens, I'm afraid.

ABBOTT: Hard or soft?

PRIESTLEY: Granite.

ABBOTT: Kiss me fuckin' Jesus.

CAMPBELL: *(Sharp.)* Abbott, I don't think it's an appropriate time or place for that sort of remark.

ABBOTT: I'm sorry, sir. It's just with my tooth acting up—

CAMPBELL: We all hate hard biscuits. We must learn to love them, because the current batch is hard. Anything else, Mr. Priestley?

PRIESTLEY: Oxo hoosh every three days in rotation. Cocoa on Fridays and Saturdays. That covers it, sir.

CAMPBELL: Questions? Fine. Assemble our biscuits, please.

               (PRIESTLEY picks out fragments and assembles them on the lid. All eyes are on him. ABBOTT scrapes at his empty bowl.)

               If I could have your attention—

               (ABBOTT stops scraping.)

               Another matter, thorny, difficult to discuss perhaps, but necessary nonetheless: social protocol during this period of confinement. There is always the question of privacy when officers and men live and work at close quarters. In the interests of naval tradition, open speech and group morale we must somehow bring privacy to this space. Don't you agree, Dr. Levick?

LEVICK: Our survival depends on it.

CAMPBELL: I would ask, therefore, that you act as if there is an invisible wall subtending this snow cave. Your side is the mess deck. You men may speak your minds freely there without fear of being overheard by any officer over here in the wardroom.

DICKASON: But, how would that work, sir?

CAMPBELL: Just as I have described it. You may say whatever you please on the other side of the invisible wall. And so may we. We will be deaf to one another, as needs require.

LEVICK: Tailor the tradition to suit the situation. Jolly good.

CAMPBELL: A direct order is still a direct order. There will be no confusion.

DICKASON: But what if I accidentally overhear you, sir?

CAMPBELL: Don't worry, Dickason. It won't happen.

               (BROWNING is watching the cookie assembly procedure like a hawk.)

BROWNING: They do look awfully hard.

ABBOTT: *(To LEVICK.)* My front tooth is beating like a drum.

LEVICK: You may have frozen the root. I'll give you some tablets.

(LEVICK opens his medicine bag.)

PRIESTLEY: *(To CAMPBELL.)* Ready.

CAMPBELL: *(To BROWNING.)* Close your eyes.

(BROWNING lies back in his bag and covers his eyes. PRIESTLEY points at the biscuits one at a time.)

PRIESTLEY: Whose biscuit is this, Rings?

BROWNING: Lieutenant Campbell.

PRIESTLEY: And this?

BROWNING: Dr. Levick.

PRIESTLEY: How about this one?

BROWNING: That's yours, sir.

PRIESTLEY: And again.

BROWNING: Dog.

PRIESTLEY: This one?

BROWNING: That's mine.

PRIESTLEY: And finally—this must be yours, Tiny.

(PRIESTLEY hands out the biscuits. ABBOTT sighs.)

CAMPBELL: Something wrong, Abbott?

(ABBOTT appears, takes his biscuit.)

ABBOTT: No sir.

(ABBOTT disappears back into his bag.)

CAMPBELL: I should like to add a final word about personal hygiene. We've been living like feral animals for

CAMPBELL: *(cont'd)* some three months now. The situation is intolerable, but there you have it. Polar travel offers few comforts. We do our best.

BROWNING: I'd freeze without my filth.

                (Laughter.)

CAMPBELL: Indeed. Well it is now clear that unsanitary conditions will prevail for at least seven more months. We must do what we can to improve the general level of personal hygiene. Case in point, the use of snow to tidy up after a bowel movement is obviously not to everyone's liking but it does serve a purpose.

BROWNING: No worry, sir. It's going to be too cold in here to smell anything.

                (More laughter.)

PRIESTLEY: Your feet, Browning. I shall, for as long as I live, never forget the smell of your feet!

BROWNING: *(Crooning.)* Roses on a summer morn—

                (Laughter continues, and builds under.)

DICKASON: I could spread his socks on toast!

PRIESTLEY: *(Singing.)* Dah-dah-dah-dah-dah-dah-dum / And call it gor-gon-zola!

CAMPBELL: Dog's appetite knows no bounds! I caught him the other morning with a seal's eyeball in his mouth.

DICKASON: A lie, sir!

ABBOTT: You ate an eye?

CAMPBELL: *(Doing DICKASON.)* A little tart in the after-taste, sir, but quite decent.

DICKASON: *(Protesting.)* Sir!

CAMPBELL: I should guard those socks with my life, Browning.

                (Much laughter.

CAMPBELL breaks spontaneously into song. The men pick it up as one. Their rendering of the hymn lifts off and soars.)

He who would valiant be / 'Gainst all disaster

ALL: Let him in constancy / Follow the Master / There's no discouragement / Shall make him once relent / His first avowed intent / To be a pilgrim. Who so beset—

CAMPBELL: Excuse me! Who is singing Pil-*grum*?

(ABBOTT, DICKASON and BROWNING put up their hands.)

Pil-*grim*. Say it.

BROWNING
& DICKASON:Pil-*grim*.

CAMPBELL: Abbott?

ABBOTT: Pil-grim.

LEVICK &
PRIESTLEY: That's the ticket! / Well done!

(CAMPBELL picks up the hymn. Everyone joins in. The energy soars again.)

ALL: Who so beset him round / With dismal stories / Do but themselves confound / His strength the more is / No foes shall stay his might / Though he with giants fight / He will make good his right / To be a pilgrim.

(DICKASON and BROWNING get it right. ABBOTT sticks with Pil-grum. A small act of defiance. CAMPBELL reaches across and shakes his foot.)

Since Lord, thou dost defend / Us with thy Spirit / We know we at the end / Shall life inherit / Then fancies flee away! / I'll fear not what men say / I'll labour night and day...

(CAMPBELL waves for everyone to stop singing.)

ABBOTT: *(Singing alone.)* To be a pil-*grum*. Ahhhh-men!

                (DICKASON starts to laugh. CAMPBELL silences him with a glance.)

CAMPBELL: My, my.

                (CAMPBELL checks his chronometer.)

                Gentlemen, lamps out in half an hour, an opportune time, I should think, for everyone to bring his journal up to date.

                (CAMPBELL and the others set about writing in their journals, each man trying to position himself close to one of the four seal oil lamps. PRIESTLEY moves a lamp, depriving LEVICK of light.)

LEVICK: If you don't mind, Lieutenant, I'd like to slightly reposition the lamp.

CAMPBELL: Go right ahead, Dr. Levick.

                (LEVICK moves the lamp. It slips off the ledge and falls into CAMPBELL's bag.)

                Dear God!

LEVICK: I'm so terribly sorry.

PRIESTLEY: It was my fault.

CAMPBELL: A pint of seal oil.

BROWNING: In the fur?

LEVICK: Where else? I'm so terribly sorry, sir.

ABBOTT: *(Croon.)* Sleeping bag for sale.

CAMPBELL: Abbott, your sense of humour frequently offends. I would ask that you curb it.

ABBOTT: Yes, sir.

CAMPBELL: I'd like to see your face when you answer me, Abbott.

                (ABBOTT sits up in his bag. He's crossed the line. No more monkey business.)

ABBOTT: Yes, sir.

CAMPBELL: We are all in His Majesty's Service. None of that
              has changed. I have no interest in booking a man
              under these conditions, but I will do as I must. I
              think we all prefer the man we knew aboard ship,
              Tiny, the strong, silent type. Wouldn't you agree,
              Mr. Priestley?

PRIESTLEY: Yes, sir.

              *(CAMPBELL turns and digs at his bag. The men
              write in their journals. ABBOTT is staring at
              PRIESTLEY. He bares his teeth. Horrified,
              PRIESTLEY crabs back out of the cave.)*

BROWNING: *(Whisper, to ABBOTT.)* No.

              (ABBOTT stands out of the cave.)

ABBOTT: Don't start in with me about authority, Browning,
              you sound like a bloody parrot.

              (Sound: ship's engine. Gulls overhead.)

              (Doing BROWNING.) 'I'm on this expedition to
              pull myself up above the crowd.' *(Normal.)* Good
              luck. Campbell cares more about the dogs. What
              did he say?

              *(BROWNING follows ABBOTT onto the deck of
              the ship, carrying a pail. He's energetic and healthy
              here, unbroken. They start to scrub deck.
              PRIESTLEY watches from the shadows.)*

BROWNING: He said: 'That decision will be made in due
              course.'

ABBOTT: They've made up their minds.

BROWNING: I would imagine.

ABBOTT: Then why don't they tell us?

BROWNING: Captain Scott wants every man giving his top push
              when we unload supplies at Hut Point.

ABBOTT: One final test.

BROWNING: If you don't like tests you shouldn't be in the south, much less thinking about going ashore. The standard is high.

ABBOTT: What standard? *(Glancing at PRIESTLEY.)* There's 'chaps' going ashore who ain't even Royal Navy.

BROWNING: *(Indicating the deck.)* That bit'll come off. Don't give me the look.

ABBOTT: Browning is a good name for you. How do you breathe?

BROWNING: You and I are on different compass headings, Tiny, that's all there is for it.

ABBOTT: Dung beetle!

BROWNING: The Royal Navy is my home, my family.

ABBOTT: Things will be different in your little family when Mr. Yexley brings in the union.

BROWNING: Not surprised his nonsense appeals to you. *(Off his look.)* You're a shit-stirrer. You ducked into the Royal Navy like a man getting out of a storm. It's like that for you, one gale after another. Me, on the other hand, I'm exactly where I ought to be. I grew up in a naval atmosphere. My father was an upper yardman. His grandfather served with Nelson.

             Saltash watermen right the way along.

ABBOTT: My father was an unemployed tin miner. So what?

BROWNING: I have a plan, this expedition is part of it. Get the rank I need. The pay packet I need. Early out, me and the missus set up a little tea shop in Cornwall. *(Naming it.)* The South Pole. Little bell over the door: da-ding, da-ding. Tourists arrive for cream tea. The missus scuttles about. I relax by the fire and tell lies about you lot. All very tidy.

ABBOTT: A tea shop? That's what you want?

             (BROWNING nods.)

             I could kill you.

BROWNING: Exactly. That's what shines through.

> (*ABBOTT scrubs in a fury.*)

It's a question of good breeding. (*Pause.*) I might as well be talking Chinese. It's not the way you think.

> (*ABBOTT grabs BROWNING's wrist, twists it playfully. Then not so playfully.*)

ABBOTT: There's things you don't know about me, Rings. Nobody on this ship does. When I was a young lambie I shared my kip with a madman. Twin brother. Slept right there, a knife in his hand on account of me father. Watched him use it once. Ear to ear.

BROWNING: We're going to the most dangerous place on earth. There's no room for your temperament.

> (*BROWNING pulls free, backs away.*)

ABBOTT: Ho-ho, you think not? (*Bared teeth.*) I will go ashore!

> (*BROWNING moves off, thoroughly spooked. ABBOTT stares down PRIESTLEY.*)
>
> *Light shift: To favour the snow cave.*
>
> *The men have blown out their lamps and withdrawn into their reindeer bags to sleep.*)

CAMPBELL: (*Drowsy.*) A lecture, Mother, you promised us a lecture.

LEVICK: Not quite prepared.

PRIESTLEY: Read from your journal.

LEVICK: Anything special?

PRIESTLEY: Breaking out of the pack.

LEVICK: (*Reading.*) December 31, 1910. Dante tells us that those who committed carnal sin are tossed about ceaselessly by the most furious winds in the second circle of hell. The corresponding hell on earth is to be found in the Southern Ocean which encircles the

LEVICK: *(cont'd)* world without break. Gale follows gale there round and round, great cyclonic storms that drive the spin of the centuries.

CAMPBELL: *(Drowsily.)* The spin of the centuries. Marvellous, Dr. Levick.

> *(Light shift: LEVICK moves away from the snow cave, transported by his memories, his eyes sky-ward. He stops to jot notes in his journal, rocking with the movement of the ship.*
>
> *PRIESTLEY looks on. ABBOTT continues to menace him.*
>
> *Sound: A flock of skuas wheels noisily overhead.)*

LEVICK: *(Reading.)* Antarktikos. It was Aristotle who named this place. No man had seen the bottom of the world, so he invented it: mysterious, remote, the last great blank on the face of the world. Geographers call such places 'sleeping beauties'. Just so. Danger and beauty entwined. World within world. A rapture both sacred and terrifying.

> *(LEVICK pauses to savour the thought.)*

Still awake, Lieutenant?

> *(CAMPBELL snores softly. LEVICK and PRIESTLEY stroll the deck.)*

It is the implacable nature of this continent that draws us here. The pure abstraction of it. Nature stripped of all complication in this half-world where physical and mental phenomena meet. Auroral displays, parhelions, lunar halos, fog bows. What would Turner have painted in such a land? In the south one is beyond the halo of art.

One is further from civilization than any human being has been since civilization began. The highest, driest, coldest desert on earth. A frost so powerful that it coagulates time itself. A four-month day, a four-month night, with four months of twilight between.

(LEVICK and PRIESTLEY part company. LEVICK sits and opens his water colours, calibrates a measurement on the horizon with his brush.)

The South Pole. Anus mundi. The puckered rectum of the world. All of it so perfectly, perfectly male. A place to set ourselves against the greatest possible emptiness. A match for the wilderness behind our eyes.

(Sound: A skua swoops low over the boat, squawking.

ABBOTT approaches LEVICK from behind.)

ABBOTT: Doing a little watercolouring, are we?

(LEVICK is in no mood for small talk.)

LEVICK: Takes a quick hand to catch it.

(ABBOTT leans close to have a look.)

ABBOTT: A beautiful place, sir.

LEVICK: Sublime. Turns the mind inward.

ABBOTT: Pardon me, sir?

(LEVICK feigns preoccupation. ABBOTT smiles, shunned again. PRIESTLEY watches from the shadows.)

I love this place, that's the truth of it. Arse-end of nowhere. There's no one *been* here. To come all this way and not go for the Pole with Captain Scott? I'd go fucking insane.

LEVICK: Hush!

(ABBOTT turns, startled.)

Look. Use your eyes.

(ABBOTT moves to the stage apron. LEVICK didn't mean to be short with the man. He moves toward him.)

LEVICK: *(cont'd)* Let it inside you, Abbott. *(Indicating the view.)* This is what you came for. Feast on it.

ABBOTT: Sir?

LEVICK: Breathe it. Feel it.

ABBOTT: It does feel better to be moving again, sir. I didn't fancy it when we were in the pack. Everything pushing in on me.

LEVICK: I'd lie in my bunk and feel the ice like a weight on my chest.

ABBOTT: And then all that bashing—

LEVICK: Such terrifying, God-like simplicity. Would you be *anywhere* else in the world, Abbott, given the choice?

ABBOTT: I'm quite happy to be here, sir.

(LEVICK sizes him up.)

LEVICK: You're going to carry this place inside you for the rest of your life, Abbott. It's going to make you bigger.

ABBOTT: Yes sir.

(LEVICK turns ABBOTT by the shoulders.)

LEVICK: There. *That's your view.* Keats wrote about the bloom on the skin of a nectarine. This is your poem, Mr. Abbott. It belongs to you.

ABBOTT: As you say, sir.

LEVICK: I should like to have you with me on Lieutenant Campbell's scientific party.

ABBOTT: Don't know much about science, sir.

LEVICK: Knowledge, that's the purpose of our pilgrimage to these frozen shores, Abbott.

ABBOTT: *(Smile.)* A pilgrimage, is it? Hm.

LEVICK: The Emperor penguin eggs I seek, Priestley and his

geological programme, all the other scientific observations, less spectacular, but gathered just as
carefully, hour by hour, in wind and drift, darkness and cold, will be striven for in order that the
modern age may have *a little more knowledge*—that
it may build on what it knows instead of what it
merely thinks.

ABBOTT: *(Not understanding.)* As you say, sir.

LEVICK: The sledges will be heavy. We need men who can
              lean into it.

ABBOTT: That's me, sir.

LEVICK: It's Lieutenant Campbell's decision but I'll put in a
              word on your behalf.

ABBOTT: I'd appreciate that, sir.

              (ABBOTT smiles, amazed at what he's pulled off.

              Light: snap to black.

              Sound: howling wind. It fades under.

              *Light shift: To favour the snow cave. The four seal
              oil lamps come up slowly. The faces of the three
              officers are visible in their bags, ABBOTT sleeps on
              his side. BROWNING is a lump in his bag.
              DICKASON's bag is empty.)*

CAMPBELL: Think in threes. Short-term. Medium-term. Long-
              term.

LEVICK: Quite right.

PRIESTLEY: Each affects the other.

LEVICK: Precisely.

CAMPBELL: Short term. We need a minimum of forty-seven
              additional seal before the light fails completely.

PRIESTLEY: And all the penguins we can muster.

LEVICK: I would ask that you remind the men that the crea-
              tures must be dead before they are butchered.

CAMPBELL: I understand your feelings, Dr. Levick. You must put them aside.

LEVICK: But—

CAMPBELL: It's a question of conserving energy. A warm animal is easier to work with.

LEVICK: We have every reason to believe that penguins feel pain as much as we do.

CAMPBELL: Point taken. Moving on.

PRIESTLEY: I'm concerned about our fuel supply.

CAMPBELL: Blubber stove. Absolutely vital.

LEVICK: Browning's your man.

CAMPBELL: He must continue his experiments.

PRIESTLEY: Ventilation could become an issue. The smitch from the lamps.

LEVICK: We shall all develop conjunctivitis. It's inevitable in these conditions.

PRIESTLEY: A chimney is always a possibility.

CAMPBELL: Out of the question. It would weaken the roof.

LEVICK: That foot and a half of snow and ice is the only thing between us and the wind. *(Pointing.)* There's already some cracking.

         (ABBOTT points at the ceiling and makes a small sizzling sound.)

CAMPBELL: I will keep a sharp eye on the situation. Of more immediate concern, we need Browning back in top nick. *(Change of tone.)* How is Browning, this morning?

BROWNING: As well as can be expected, sir.

CAMPBELL: We'd like to see you up and about today, Browning.

BROWNING: I'll do my best, sir.

CAMPBELL: *(Change of tone.)* Medium term. Dr. Levick, other medical concerns?

LEVICK: In my view the chief enemy is mental torpor. I have read medical accounts of the Greeley expedition. The men were sleeping sixteen hours a day.

CAMPBELL: Americans. Survival of the fittest and all that rubbish. No room for honour or feeling there. It's no wonder they ended badly.

LEVICK: They kept the spark of life alive at the cost of life itself.

CAMPBELL: Well put.

LEVICK: I met one of the men who'd been with Greeley.

PRIESTLEY: No.

LEVICK: At the Royal Geographical Society. There was a smoker for him.

CAMPBELL: Cannibals at the Royal Society? What a travesty.

ABBOTT: What did he have to say for himself?

CAMPBELL: The invisible wall, Abbott! You can't hear us.

LEVICK: He was a gnarled little fellow by then—

CAMPBELL: Gentlemen, the Greeley expedition offers us no model. May we move on?

LEVICK: Suffice to say I shall be monitoring the mental health of the party.

CAMPBELL: Long term.

    (Long silence.)

Issues? Problems? Reflections?

    (More silence. The officers close their eyes. BROWNING opens his, a haunted stare. CAMPBELL sits up, startled by something in his bag. He covers.)

PRIESTLEY: I'm afraid it—it's too taxing to contemplate, sir.

(Sound: wind burst.

DICKASON enters the snow cave through the tunnel.)

DICKASON: Blowing like stink. Pebbles whizzing round like musket shot. Couldn't make it to the anemometer.

LEVICK: Moderate gale?

DICKASON: Strong gale, sir.

(LEVICK makes a note in his journal. CAMPBELL is restless in his bag, something is bothering him.)

The cache was completely drifted over.

CAMPBELL: We shall come back to long-term issues in due course. Abbott—

ABBOTT: Sir.

CAMPBELL: Your food cache was a disaster.

ABBOTT: It was double-walled, sir.

CAMPBELL: Go higher up the moraine. Make sure there's an easy path. We must be able to find it in white-out conditions.

ABBOTT: What about helping Dickason with the hoosh, sir?

CAMPBELL: *(To DICKASON.)* You do all the cooking until our stores are secure. *(To PRIESTLEY.)* I want the hoosh ration cut by half until our meat supply is secure.

(ABBOTT crawls out of his sleeping bag and heads for the tunnel. DICKASON is ready to chop up the frozen penguin with an axe.)

DICKASON: I need a proper chopping block, sir. *(Indicating stone floor.)* Ruin the edge on this.

CAMPBELL: Browning.

BROWNING: Sir.

CAMPBELL: Go to Hell's Gate moraine and pick up one of the empty crates we cached there.

BROWNING: To Hell's Gate, sir?

DICKASON: I can handle that, sir. I like getting ragged out.

CAMPBELL: Browning needs a task. Off we go, Browning.

DICKASON: It's blowing fifty knots, sir.

> (*CAMPBELL looks sharply at DICKASON. DICKASON sets about filing his axe.*)

CAMPBELL: Come on, Browning! Up-up-up! Mind over matter!

BROWNING: Aye-aye, sir.

> (*BROWNING follows ABBOTT out.*)

ABBOTT: Come on, Rings. I'll point you.

CAMPBELL: Let the man manage himself.

> (*ABBOTT and BROWNING complete their exit. There is an uncomfortable pause. CAMPBELL fidgets restlessly in his bag.*
>
> *Sound: DICKASON sharpens his axe.*)

CAMPBELL: Plato said the good ruler is a reluctant man.

PRIESTLEY: Indeed.

CAMPBELL: Browning has allowed a condition of general weakness to cloud his thinking. Wouldn't you say, Dr. Levick?

LEVICK: To a degree.

CAMPBELL: (*To DICKASON.*) Brew up for Browning's return.

DICKASON: Aye-aye, sir.

> (*CAMPBELL checks his chronometer.*)

CAMPBELL: Mr. Priestley, I should like you to find an appropriate station for the anemometer. (*To LEVICK.*) We must strive to maintain continuity in our meteorological observations.

LEVICK: An absolute must.

(PRIESTLEY exits the cave on his hands and knees.)

CAMPBELL: Bugger be damned.

LEVICK: What's the matter?

CAMPBELL: *(Confidential.)* I have wet myself.

LEVICK: I think it's happened to all of us.

CAMPBELL: You've had an episode?

LEVICK: Two nights ago. Seal makes the urine overly acidic. The kidneys can't retain that level of toxicity, which, coupled with our general exhaustion, results in involuntary micturition.

(CAMPBELL swats at his clothes.)

CAMPBELL: I'm afraid I really can't put up with this! You must do something.

LEVICK: Nothing to be done, unfortunately.

CAMPBELL: Seven months in these clothes.

LEVICK: We'll just have to hope our systems adjust.

CAMPBELL: The stench!

LEVICK: Your mind will have to adjust as well as your organs of digestion.

CAMPBELL: The filth!

LEVICK: You are a meticulous man, Lieutenant. Order is your watchword. Cleanliness your obsession. And here we are. As the medical man on this expedition it's my job to keep an eye on just such a situation. *(Pause.)* Mental strain, sir. We must nip it in the bud.

CAMPBELL: Indeed.

(Long pause. The sound of DICKASON whetting his axe.)

Was I wrong to send the man out?

LEVICK: Hell's Gate is almost a mile. Fifty knots of wind.

DICKASON: I'll go out after him.

CAMPBELL: No. That won't be necessary. Each man must be prepared to carry the weight of the group. It can't be any other way. Browning's example will lift us all.

LEVICK: As you say, sir.

CAMPBELL: Weakness spreads like a cancer. Dickie and I know these waters. Norway. Remember, Dickie?

DICKASON: (*Nervous.*) Aye, sir. I do.

               (*LIGHT SHIFT: To favour DICKASON, filing his axe. CAMPBELL appears from the gloom, tottering with drink.*)

CAMPBELL: Dickason?

               (*DICKASON comes to his feet, steps out of the snow cave.*)

DICKASON: Yes sir.

CAMPBELL: Shh. A word.

DICKASON: Sir?

CAMPBELL: Difficult times.

DICKASON: It's a new place, sir. We're all making adjustments.

               (*Sound: a woman's wail.*)

CAMPBELL: Is that what you call it?

               (*CAMPBELL drinks, wobbles unsteadily.*)

               Empty space. That's what I like about fjord country. Away from it all. England. Bloody Royal Navy. Gone-gone-gone.

               (*CAMPBELL drinks. Smiles.*)

               How are you?

DICKASON: I'm fine, sir.

CAMPBELL: Have you, by any chance, been talking to Mrs. Campbell?

DICKASON: Sir?

CAMPBELL: She seeks allies, Dickie. Divide my house against itself. Her strategy, you see. *(Pause.)* Have you?

             (DICKASON is caught out.)

             We've been through worse, Dickie. The truth.

DICKASON: She called me into her rooms, sir.

CAMPBELL: What did she talk to you about?

DICKASON: She…she asked me to stop the wind, sir.

             (CAMPBELL laughs hideously.)

CAMPBELL: Stop the wind! Of course! *(Her voice.)* I hear demon voices!

             (CAMPBELL laughs again.

             Sound: woman's wail.)

             It's a tactic, that's my view. Play madness.

             (CAMPBELL puts his arm around DICKASON's shoulder.)

             I'm drawing a circle round us, Dickie. Will you stand with me?

DICKASON: I'll do whatever you ask, sir.

CAMPBELL: That's my man. Less said, soonest mended. Drink?

             (DICKASON takes a drink.)

             One bloody thing after another. Had a letter from the old man this morning. Can't believe I've retired from the service. He accuses me of running away.

DICKASON: He would take it hard, sir. The sea is his life.

CAMPBELL: Commander of the bloody Royal yacht. Glorified taxi driver for the monarch, nothing more.

(*CAMPBELL drinks again.*)

Used to make me help him build bloody scale models. *H.M.S. Terror* under full canvas, inch to the foot! Painting tiny emblems on tiny sleeves. Moving men around the deck with tweezers! Drake! Raleigh! Cook!

(*CAMPBELL mimics the activity and cackles with laughter.*)

You and I have other fish to fry.

(*Sound: more wind. The woman wails and moans.*)

I have been invited to accompany Captain Scott to Antarctica. He wants me to command the expedition's scientific arm.

DICKASON: (*Awe.*) That's quite an honour, sir.

CAMPBELL: Indeed. Thousands of people ready to sign up. Schoolchildren all over Britain are collecting shillings. Bad timing, of course. Unless I can convince myself that Mrs. Campbell will sort herself out in my absence.

(*Sound: The wail.*)

(*Drinks.*) What do you think, my man?

DICKASON: I don't know, sir. It's tricky, isn't it?

CAMPBELL: It looks a sure thing. We're going to plant the Jack at the South Pole.

DICKASON: You'll encounter some winds to fly it in down there, sir.

(*Sound: more wind. The woman cries, off.*)

CAMPBELL: *We*, Dickason. What do you think?

DICKASON: Sir?

CAMPBELL: I shall want you with me.

DICKASON: I'd be greatly honoured, sir.

CAMPBELL: This is once in a lifetime stuff. Be like turning down a chance with Drake or Raleigh. I must simply announce to her that I'm going. It can't be any other way.

> *(Sound: another wail.)*

Never easy with these things. Always people left behind.

> *(Sound: the woman's cry becomes a wind of building intensity.)*

We're going to the South Pole, Dickason. The last great emptiness will be claimed by an Englishman.

> *(CAMPBELL puts his hands on DICKASON's shoulders. A moment of awkward affection.)*

You're a trustworthy man, Dickie. You can hold a secret. I like that.

> *(CAMPBELL and DICKASON go into a freeze.*
>
> *Sound: the wind howls.*
>
> *Light shift: snow squall.*
>
> *CAMPBELL and DICKASON cling to each other in a hurricane burst.)*

CAMPBELL: Hold on!

DICKASON: Get down!

CAMPBELL: We'll never find him in this!

DICKASON: *(Pointing.)* The moraine!

CAMPBELL: Can't see ten feet!

> *(BROWNING crawls into view, fighting the same wind, dragging a wooden crate. He is bareheaded, in a hypothermic stupor.*
>
> *SOUND: The wind subsides.)*

CAMPBELL: Browning!

(CAMPBELL and DICKASON set about warming him.)

BROWNING: *(Mad babble.)* No cause for alarm, SIR! Pull as one, SIR!

CAMPBELL: Where is your hat?

BROWNING: A miracle, sir! God sent us a leopard seal!

DICKASON: Where?

BROWNING: On the flow edge! Sound asleep! I crept up on me belly! I killed him with my ski pole!

(BROWNING cackles like a madman.)

CAMPBELL: Bravo, Browning!

DICKASON: You're a hard man, Rings!

BROWNING: Wait! That's not the end! When I gutted him I found these—

(BROWNING displays the contents of his wooden crate. Handfuls of beautiful shining fish.)

Undigested fish. Thirty-six of'em!

DICKASON: We shall have a feast!

(CAMPBELL and DICKASON hug BROWNING and carry him to the cave.)

(Singing.) "And to those who will not merry merry be / We'll never share our joy"

DICKASON &
CAMPBELL: "Sing, sing the boys in blue / Have won the victory / And if ever I return again / And if ever I return again/ "

(Light: cross-fade to the cave.

The company settle into their bags.)

ALL: *(Singing.)* "And if ever I return again / I'll make you my bride."

(Sound: the company strikes a triumphant tableau and hums "The Fading of the Light".

Light shift: to PRIESTLEY in his chair. He reads from his journal.)

PRIESTLEY: April 12, 1912. A red letter day in our gastronomical calendar and we spent a very jovial evening in consequence, our happiness secured by the weakest man in the party.

(DICKASON studies the tableau.)

DICKASON: Dear little Browning…

(Light fades on snow cave.)

PRIESTLEY: *(Reading.)* We sit together round a single guttering candle and invent a mental game to defy the wildest extreme of nature.

(Light: a single candle burns in the cave.)

DICKASON: So snug, Mr. Nipcheese. *(Whisper.)* Muscatel. Muscatel.

PRIESTLEY: Pure invention, Dickie.

(Sound: end humming.

Light: the last candle is blown out in the tableau.

PRIESTLEY begins to tremble.)

PRIESTLEY: I remember how the loss of a single biscuit crumb left a sense of personal injury which lingered for a week. How the greatest friends were so much on each other's nerves that they did not speak for days for fear of the consequences. That prowling danger behind another man's eyes. *(Pause.)* You have forgotten the real game, Dickie…how we warmed our hands on the fiercest fires of Hell.

(The darker memory washes into DICKASON's face.

Light shift: the hearth light source glows up into a raging inferno. PRIESTLEY and DICKASON look up into the flames. Fear and wonder.

Snap to black.

End of ACT ONE.)

ACT TWO

(Lights up: on PRIESTLEY, dozing in his chair. The tremble evident.)

PRIESTLEY: One…endless…day…

(Lights cross-fade to low levels.

Sound: the wind builds to katabatic force.

CAMPBELL comes into view. His tattered trousers are at his knees and he can't get them up as he fights to protect himself from the wind.)

CAMPBELL: *(To the Gods.)* Glory in adversity! Splendour in misfortune! A harvest of joy raised upon a battlefield of suffering!

(CAMPBELL stumbles into the cave. Drunk with cold.

Light shift: to favour LEVICK. Everyone else is asleep. CAMPBELL falls panting and gasping into his bag. He and LEVICK converse in whispers.)

LEVICK: Loose motion?

CAMPBELL: Explosive, I'm afraid.

LEVICK: Dear-dear-dear.

CAMPBELL: The wind blew me down. I got frost nip on my nethers.

LEVICK: Buttocks?

CAMPBELL: The entire region.

(CAMPBELL groans with rage and despair.)

Oh Lord, I've soiled myself.

LEVICK: Give them to me.

CAMPBELL: I—I can't bear this.

LEVICK: Yes you can.

CAMPBELL: The filth! The stench!

LEVICK: My bag smells like a loo in the Cairo train station.

CAMPBELL: *(Childlike.)* I can't live like an animal. I shall go mad.

LEVICK: *(Firm.)* Nonsense. These are *our* smells. We must learn to love them.

> *(CAMPBELL hands his pants out of his bag.)*

Your chronometer is missing.

> *(LEVICK holds up the broken lanyard. ABBOTT opens his eyes.)*

CAMPBELL: Good God.

LEVICK: Not to worry.

CAMPBELL: Our overland journey to Hut Point. The navigation tables.

LEVICK: We'll follow the coastline.

CAMPBELL: We're heading into months of pitch black! We won't know if it's day or night.

LEVICK: We'll count the days.

CAMPBELL: How? Without an objective reference—

LEVICK: When you go to sleep it is night. When you awaken it is the morning of the next day.

CAMPBELL: Well, I'm awake now.

LEVICK: Ergo, it is morning.

CAMPBELL: *(To the men.)* Eight bells. Rise and shine. Rise and shine. The day is fine! Show a leg! Mr. Priestley?

PRIESTLEY: Here, sir.

>*(The men rise from their bags one by one.)*

CAMPBELL: Dickason.

DICKASON: Sir.

CAMPBELL: Browning.

BROWNING: *(Weak.)* Aye.

CAMPBELL: Abbott.

ABBOTT: Good morning, gentlemen.

>*(We hold the visual. The men have all been visibly transformed by their confinement. Filthy with a mixture of soot and seal fat. Matted hair and beards. Clothing in tatters.*
>
>*ABBOTT has a bandage under his jaw. DICKASON wears an eyepatch. He sets about lighting lamps.*
>
>*CAMPBELL obsessively grooms the fur in his sleeping bag. He is still juddering from the cold.)*

CAMPBELL: How is Browning this morning?

BROWNING: A bit low, sir.

CAMPBELL: Abbott, status of the gums?

ABBOTT: Rotting meat, sir.

LEVICK: I'm prepared to lance the abcess if need be.

CAMPBELL: *(To DICKASON.)* Your conjunctivitis?

DICKASON: The ointment seems to have brought it round, sir.

CAMPBELL: Other physical problems?

PRIESTLEY: I appear to have a sore opening up on my right buttock.

LEVICK: I'll apply some zinc.

CAMPBELL: Very well, then. Peggies today, Abbott and

Dickason. Mug up at eleven-hundred. Yes, Browning—

BROWNING: If I might, sir. I had another dream which I would like to recount to Dr. Levick while it is still fresh a'mind.

DICKASON: Sheep's tongue and cheese on a slab of fresh bread.

BROWNING: Nothing to do with food.

> (Catcalls and jibes. "Another bloody feast / Slurping it up.")

LEVICK: Hear the man out. It does him good.

> (CAMPBELL obsesses, picking the filth out of his sleeping bag.)

BROWNING: There was a father with three sons in a grand country house. Turrets and battlements like a great medieval fortress. I was the middle son.

> (Jeers from DICKASON and ABBOTT. "A rich boy / Beats the tea shop." LEVICK is taking notes in his journal.)

LEVICK: Go on.

BROWNING: Folk was making a fuss, preparing me for some kind of ceremony. There was an elaborate suit that belonged to my father. I was to wear it but the rig didn't fit properly. A tailor was seeing to the crotch of my trousers with a mouthful of pins.

LEVICK: Mm-hm. Describe this suit.

BROWNING: An officer's dress jacket, sir, with a blue velvet sash and a great wad of medals. Fit for a king, it was.

> (LEVICK takes notes. CAMPBELL grooms his bag more obsessively. He's not comfortable with this talk.)

LEVICK: Go on.

BROWNING: Me and me brothers were preparing for the feast and—

DICKASON: Here comes the tiddy oggies and mutton chops.

BROWNING: The food wasn't even in it.

LEVICK: The feast would follow the ceremony?

BROWNING: Exactly, sir. Now comes the strangeness of it. My
             eldest brother had grown a tail and the three of us
             was examining it, trying to decide if we should tell
             our father about this tail or hide it from him. He
             was a fierce man, you see, and we was all deathly
             afraid of his temper.

LEVICK: What sort of tail?

BROWNING: Like a lizard's tail, sir. Thick and scaly. It kind of
             hung out of his bum.

CAMPBELL: We pray for your bowels to move, Browning.

             (Laughter.)

LEVICK: Interesting.

BROWNING: What does it mean, sir?

CAMPBELL: That dream is the voice of undigested seal meat.

             *(More laughter. CAMPBELL grooms his bag with a
             vengeance.)*

LEVICK: Let's have a go. The father's jacket with the sash
             and medals, fit for a king, you said. A cloak of
             office, if you will. Rings dons the magic robe and
             thereby supplants his father. But first, a ceremony,
             a trial by fire. The man at his crotch with the
             mouthful of pins is a kind of witch doctor.

ABBOTT: *(To BROWNING.)* Oooga-booga!

             (BROWNING startles. Laughter.)

             What about the lizard tail?

LEVICK: We'll have to think about that.

CAMPBELL: Very well, then, gentlemen, if we could move on. I
             have been thinking. It's May the first. We've done
             rather well, all things considered.

LEVICK: Thanks be to the Almighty.

PRIESTLEY: Hear, hear.

CAMPBELL: It will be another four months before light returns sufficiently for us to begin our overland trek to rejoin Captain Scott's party at Hut Point.

DICKASON: Picture them there now. All snug. The coal stove chuffing away.

BROWNING: Toasting their triumph at the Pole.

CAMPBELL: Worried sick about us, no doubt.

PRIESTLEY: What if Amundsen won the race?

LEVICK: Don't talk nonsense.

CAMPBELL: Gentlemen, our own triumph over these appalling conditions will be no less heroic than Captain Scott's achievement at the Pole.

LEVICK: We are writing history for the Modern Age.

CAMPBELL: Spot on. We've set a fine example. *(Pause.)* Now it's time to raise the bar!

                (ABBOTT begins to scrape his bowl. Tink-a-tink-a-tink.)

                My principal concern at this juncture is that a kind of lethargy may overtake us inch by inch. Dr. Levick?

LEVICK: There is an oppressive gloom that prolonged indolence induces. I would characterize it as a tone of morbidity that may infiltrate our thinking and strangle our collective will.

BROWNING: That sounds bloody awful.

CAMPBELL: Abbott.

                (ABBOTT stops scraping his bowl.)

DICKASON: *(To LEVICK.)* I don't follow, sir. This gloom—

ABBOTT: They don't want you to go crackers.

BROWNING: Bit late in the day!

               (The men share a great laugh. CAMPBELL and LEVICK exchange a look.)

CAMPBELL: The brain is a muscle! We must exercise it!

               (Silence.)

               I have revised our daily plan. A more rigorous schedule, gentlemen! On the whole, an uncomfortable ship is a safe ship. If we want safety our minds must be on wires of steel! Please listen carefully. These are my new orders. Browning, Dickason and Priestley will henceforth take anemometer and temperature readings at six in the morning and six in the evening, no matter the weather. Dr. Levick will continue to maintain the log.

LEVICK: A precise meteorological record for this region. It would be a magnificent achievement.

CAMPBELL: Another laurel wreath for the expedition.

PRIESTLEY: Done!

CAMPBELL: That's my lad! Henceforth there will be a general meeting each morning immediately following mug-up. In the short term our focus must be on improving the efficiency of the blubber stove. Browning—

BROWNING: Sir?

CAMPBELL: You have the ability to visualize mechanical things in dimension. We look to you for design improvements.

BROWNING: Soon as I get my strength back, sir.

CAMPBELL: No, Browning! This problem will not wait. Your health depends upon its resolution. In this regard, daily exercise and fresh air must become a priority. I should like to see you out of doors sharpening up your semaphore skills, half-an-hour, every day.

BROWNING: Yes sir.

CAMPBELL: Abbott.

                (No response.)

                Abbott?

BROWNING: I think he's drifted off, sir.

                (CAMPBELL grabs ABBOTT's foot and shakes it roughly.)

CAMPBELL: Important things are being discussed here, Abbott.

ABBOTT: I'm listening, sir.

CAMPBELL: I want the sledge and the specimen boxes kept clear of snow. I was out there this morning and it's all badly drifted over.

ABBOTT: Everything is double-wanded, sir. There's no chance of it going missing.

CAMPBELL: That is hardly the point. Our survival depends on that sledge and its provisions. Our scientific achievement resides in the specimen boxes. I want it all in top nick! The drift cleared, by you, every day!

ABBOTT: Aye-aye.

CAMPBELL: I don't like your tone of voice, Abbott. Much of this new routine is for your benefit.

ABBOTT: As you say, sir.

CAMPBELL: Sit up in your bag.

                (ABBOTT does as he is told.)

                Next, the question of fresh meat. I want a hunting party on the seafront each and every afternoon. Abbott to lead as he has the surer hand with the killing stave, Browning, Dickason and Priestley to accompany him in rotation.

DICKASON: No matter if it's blowing, sir?

CAMPBELL: I know they are scarce in this season but we must look.

PRIESTLEY: As you know, we're down to three animals and one of them is small.

(Pause.)

LEVICK: Dear, dear.

CAMPBELL: An equally pressing concern is the whole matter of personal hygiene. I know we are all trying but we must try harder. I want every man outside first thing in the morning for a freshener. Scour the face in the nearest snowbank. Scrub the hands. No matter if nothing seems to be accomplished. Do it!

Other matters, to leaven the day and lift us from our toil, Dr. Levick has offered to provide evening lectures and poetry readings from time to time. Human physiology. Nutrition. Perhaps some talks on his research into the Emperor penguin.

DICKASON: Lectures about penguins, sir?

LEVICK: The Emperor is the most primitive bird in existence. We know the embryo recapitulates the former lives of a species. It's my hope that upon proper study the eggs I've collected will establish a link between birds and reptiles.

BROWNING: I'll look forward to that Dr. Levick.

CAMPBELL: Mr. Priestley has suggested we form a debating society.

PRIESTLEY: Calisthenics for the mind.

(BROWNING releases a long fart. Groans.)

LEVICK: Well done, Browning. Keep them coming.

CAMPBELL: We shall institute the debating society as soon as we can agree on a worthy subject.

PRIESTLEY: Perhaps we could leave that to the men.

CAMPBELL: Fine idea! You chaps come up with some topics.

DICKASON: Things to argue about, sir?

LEVICK: Reasoned argument sharpens the mind, Dickie.

CAMPBELL: These are my new orders! I trust we will all be busy.

DICKASON: Effective immediately, sir?

CAMPBELL: Everybody out for a freshener!

(Light shift.

Sound: katabatic wind.

BROWNING and ABBOTT flop out of the cave. BROWNING clings to ABBOTT in the gale. They must assume the 'flying posture' flat on their bellies.

Sound: the wind subsides.)

ABBOTT: He's lost his mind. There's no seals for ten thousand miles.

(BROWNING starts to practise his semaphore.)

Did you hear him in the night? *(Doing CAMPBELL.)* My chronometer! The filth! I shall go mad! Picking at the fur in his bag like a bloody baboon.

(BROWNING continues his semaphore exercises. Resolute.)

He's come unstrung, that's what I think. *(Smirk.)* Maybe you have too.

BROWNING: There's a logic to his command. I wouldn't expect you to understand.

(ABBOTT turns away with a sneer and begins to clear blocks of snow from the sledge.)

ABBOTT: I subscribe to Mr. Yexley's views. The lower deck is one great combustible mass, one flashpoint and the whole Royal Navy bursts into flame.

BROWNING: You'd feel different if you were building a career in it.

ABBOTT: *(Disgust.)* Look at you...

(BROWNING signals with greater vigour, mouthing the letters.)

Weak as a rat, sucking on a sugar cube every other Sunday…and there's this lot…

(ABBOTT indicates food on the sledge.)

BROWNING: We must hold supplies back for the overland journey.

> *(ABBOTT pulls loose a tin of biscuits. Offers one to BROWNING. BROWNING semaphores, trying to ignore him.)*

ABBOTT: Eat it!

BROWNING: NO! Put it back or I'll report you.

ABBOTT: Are you prepared to follow this idiot to your grave?

BROWNING: You've got a poison in you, Abbott.

ABBOTT: Oh, that I do. My mouth is a volcano of pus! And whose fault is that?

> *(BROWNING goes down to one knee, gasping with a cramp.)*

His journal! Have you looked?

BROWNING: Of course not!

ABBOTT: Pencil sketches of the bleeding hills! He's a schoolboy peeking over the garden wall. He's not fit to lead men in a place like this.

BROWNING: I take my cue from Dr. Levick. He's a man of some intelligence and—

ABBOTT: Levick served on the *Essex*! Cambridge arse crawlers top to bottom. Talk of the China station, it was. *H.M.S. Nancy Boy*.

BROWNING: The doctor has a wife.

ABBOTT: Oh, they've all got their wives, don't they? Levick's the bastard that hooked me into this! I was bound for the Pole with Scott!

BROWNING: You were lucky to get ashore at all.

ABBOTT: And you'll be lucky to get home.

(*ABBOTT displays the chronometer, hung on its lanyard. He sways it back and forth like a hypnotist. BROWNING is horrified.*)

BROWNING: Where'd you get that?

ABBOTT: (*Whisper.*) Found it in the drift. Someone has to know what day it is.

(*BROWNING cringes away. ABBOTT pushes in.*)

Look around. There's your fucking view! A pitch-black hellhole at the end of the fucking earth! I will not die for them!

(*ABBOTT bares his teeth, his face a demon mask. BROWNING is seized with cramp. He howls. ABBOTT watches him.*)

I choose to look at things as they are, Rings. A live donkey is better than a dead lion. You shouldn't be out in this. You could die...and God only knows what Campbell would have us do with you then. (*Doing CAMPBELL.*) May I have the brisket saw, please!

BROWNING: No!

(*ABBOTT puts his arm around BROWNING's shoulder.*)

ABBOTT: You'll have your tea shop, Rings. I'm not going to let you die. But when the time comes I'm going to look for you to stand by me. It may be that you and I are the only ones who fully grasp our situation.

(*Sound: wind builds.*

Light shift. ABBOTT withdraws.

BROWNING is alone now.)

BROWNING: The real situation is that a land crab has hatched inside my body. I have told no one, because of the alarm that will be caused but the fact is sure. On the voyage down we stopped at South Trinidad Island, a little speck stuck out in the mid-Atlantic. Dr. Levick wanted to collect specimens. Lashly, Evans, Cherry and me manned the oars to take him ashore.

> *(Light shift: LEVICK sits in the vanishing point. He sketches in his journal, lost in thought.)*

Lashly and Cherry rowed back to the ship as there was nowhere to beach the pinnace. The main thing about this island was the vast number of land crabs on the premises.

Like huge spiders, they were, scuttling about on their spiny legs. Eyes on long stalks. They had no fear of us. Surrounded us wherever we went, they did. Watching with their twitchy eyes. Little fingers grooming their mouths. Like they were waiting for something which they knew about and we didn't. *(Animal voice.)* Just die. We'll do the rest.

> *(LEVICK takes a fern frond that's pressed flat in the pages of his journal, studies it against the light.)*

We worked like demons collecting specimens and Dr. Levick was very excited about the findings. *(Pride.)* I personally collected a new species of fern. Late in the afternoon the boat come back for us but the swell was such they couldn't safely come ashore. There was nothing for it but to swim to them.

Evans went first and in a trice the man was fighting for his life. *(To LEVICK.)* Sir, the swell is sucking him back toward the rocks! He'll be dashed to bits!

It was a moment of real panic but there was nothing to be done. Dr. Levick behaved just as the best sort of Englishman does in such a situation. He was worried looking but he never said nothing out of the way. He sat down at the top of a rock and ate a biscuit in the coolest manner possible.

He did not want that biscuit. It was a lesson not to panic. He knew I saw and understood. It was a bond between us.

(*LEVICK eats his biscuit. BROWNING semaphores.*)

Evans was finally rescued and it was established through signals that Dr. Levick and I would remain ashore, in hopes of calmer conditions the following day.

We banked a huge bonfire to warm ourselves and keep the land crabs at bay, but it only seemed to attract them. They stood at the edge of our light. I tried to stay awake but I was stove in and there was no fighting it. That's when it happened, when both of us was fast in sleep.

A female come forward on her spidery legs and deposited her egg in my mouth. A male then scuttled forward to fertilize it, other crabs moving close to watch. A dark and evil nativity, it was.

I was aware of nothing except a terrible thirst in the morning.

(*BROWNING moves back into the cave. Doubles up with a cramp.*)

There's no avoiding it now. A story is being told within me.

(*Light shift: To favour the cave. CAMPBELL picks at his sleeping bag. PRIESTLEY writes in his journal. DICKASON hacks meat from a frozen penguin with a hatchet. ABBOTT smokes and stares at the ceiling, points a finger and makes his sizzling sound. BROWNING snores, his body position encroaching on ABBOTT. ABBOTT sits up in his bag, pushes BROWNING away. He watches DICKASON work. Calculating.*)

CAMPBELL: Real explorers don't poach on one another's declared territory. Amundsen announced an expedition to the North Pole and then came south. He

CAMPBELL: *(cont'd)* sailed down here on a lie and he will fail at the Pole.

>   *(ABBOTT whispers to DICKASON. Their conversation continues, under. A sense of negotiation.)*

PRIESTLEY: There is the factor of his dogs, sir.

>   *(CAMPBELL picks up his sextant and starts to polish.)*

CAMPBELL: *(Disgust.)* They eat them, Mr. Priestley. There is an image you must hold in your mind. The Norwegian boiling up the head of his favourite dog. That's the kind of barbarians we're dealing with here. Dog brains for breakfast. *(To the men.)* What's all this then?

>   *(ABBOTT is caught out.)*

ABBOTT: I want to trade places with Dickason, sir.

CAMPBELL: Why?

ABBOTT: To be closer to the mouth of the tunnel, sir.

CAMPBELL: Dickason is popping in and out all day long to fetch items we need from the sledge.

ABBOTT: It's just that I have a slight problem with my breathing, sir. Tucked back in the corner, everything pressing in on me.

CAMPBELL: We are all making adjustments, Abbott. Do your best.

>   *(Pause. DICKASON chops at his frozen penguin. ABBOTT lies back in his bag and smokes. He fidgets, drumming on his chest.)*

CAMPBELL: *(To PRIESTLEY.)* I don't mean to be short with you, Mr. Priestley. There's an element of Royal Navy tradition to all these questions. It may be hard for you to grasp the nuances.

ABBOTT: Can you tell me what time it is, sir?

CAMPBELL: Eleven hundred hours.

(CAMPBELL sets about resecuring his sextant in a canvas sack.)

PRIESTLEY: I'm not really part of the family, so to speak.

CAMPBELL: Nonsense. You fit in beautifully.

PRIESTLEY: Thank you, sir, but I've no real qualifications except my aunt's friendship with Sir Clements Markham. Never been a hundred miles from home, never pitched a tent!

(BROWNING groans in his bag. ABBOTT smokes and drums on his chest.)

CAMPBELL: The only real qualification is an appetite for hardship.

PRIESTLEY: I suppose that's what I wanted, sir, having read my Conrad. A young man seeks his crucible.

CAMPBELL: *(Handing his sextant.)* Dickason, if you would. I think geology will prove to be a good vocation for you, Mr. Priestley.

PRIESTLEY: I don't really care about rocks, sir. Geology lets me roam the hills and consider the questions that really interest me. *(Pause.)* There is a larger project to my thinking, you see…

CAMPBELL: Oh? What would that be?

PRIESTLEY: It all sounds rather pretentious, really…

CAMPBELL: Come, come, don't be shy.

PRIESTLEY: I want to understand…time, sir. *(ABBOTT snorts.)* Learn how to take it apart and put it back together again. Human time, I mean. The clock of the soul.

(ABBOTT makes a small ticking sound.)

CAMPBELL: Well, well, well. *(Pause.)* Perhaps you should be writing novels like Mr. Conrad.

PRIESTLEY: *(Pride.)* Someday, sir.

(CAMPBELL reappraises PRIESTLEY.

DICKASON takes the sextant over to his side of the cave.)

CAMPBELL: Oh, I see it all now. A young chap's adventures out back of beyond. You'll dine out on it for years. *(Confidential.)* Nothing attracts the young ladies like a bit of foreign rip-roar.

(They laugh.)

PRIESTLEY: It's you who will hold them spellbound, sir.

CAMPBELL: *(Pick-up line, years hence.)* Yes, my dear, we ate our boots...and danced on the head of a pin.

(CAMPBELL leans close to whisper a dirty aside. He and PRIESTLEY laugh.)

PRIESTLEY: *(Laughing.)* They'll swoon!

CAMPBELL: Married man. Unfortunately.

(DICKASON is looking at CAMPBELL. CAMPBELL catches his eye. DICKASON looks away.)

I wonder what you'll make of all this, when you look back years from now.

PRIESTLEY: I shall remember your command, sir. The way you handled the men.

(PRIESTLEY shoots a look at ABBOTT.)

CAMPBELL: It's my job to remind them of their best qualities. One must shape the experience. Give it a context. A resonance.

PRIESTLEY: Something to hold on to.

CAMPBELL: I'll tell you what I'll hold on to. Dickason, here. Gold. Pure, shining, unalloyed.

DICKASON: Thank you, sir.

CAMPBELL: *(Irritation.)* The invisible wall, Dickie. You can't hear me.

DICKASON: Apologies, sir.

CAMPBELL: Dickie's got Abbott whispering in his ear. We must keep a sharp eye. He may forget which side his bread is buttered on.

(DICKASON is stung by the remark.)

ABBOTT: *(Whisper.)* You can't hear him, Dog.

CAMPBELL: Don't sit there slack-jawed, Dickie. Make yourself useful, the cooking area is filthy.

(DICKASON sets about tidying up. ABBOTT lights a cigarette from his lamp.)

PRIESTLEY: Thankfully we seem to be getting on rather well.

CAMPBELL: Things are simple here. That's the beauty of it. All I need do to break a man is put him outside the circle. Let him stand out there in the wind and do some thinking about the benefits of my command. Smartness and silence are the hallmarks of an efficient ship. I think the men know that and that is why we get along. *(Pause.)* Keep up the journal, Priestley. Let this cave be your crucible.

PRIESTLEY: The back of the chronometer is already off, so to speak. I'm looking into the workings.

ABBOTT: Tick. Tick. Tick. Tick.

CAMPBELL: Let me know when you figure out what makes our friend in the corner go 'round and 'round.

(ABBOTT smiles.)

See the way he fidgets? Sure sign that a man has another man inside him. Someone he doesn't want us to see. No worry. We shall get down to brass tacks before we're done here. Off you go, Dickason, fetch us some fresh snow for the hoosh.

(DICKASON exits.)

PRIESTLEY: I shall remember these days for the rest of my life, sir.

CAMPBELL: You watch, everything will blend together. One endless day. A few well-practised anecdotes to

CAMPBELL: *(cont'd)* fudge over the nasty bits, the rest pure invention.

                 (BROWNING awakes with a sudden flail and sits bolt upright.)

ABBOTT: Easy does it, Rings.

BROWNING: *(In a panic.)* Doctor? Doctor?

CAMPBELL: He's fetching medical supplies from the sledge.

BROWNING: I've had another of my dreams, sir. I can't close my eyes but they come rushing in upon me.

CAMPBELL: Calm down, Browning.

PRIESTLEY: What sort of dream?

ABBOTT: Not the chap with the lizard tail sticking out his arse, I hope.

BROWNING: It was the father and the three sons again, sir, only this time I dreamt of the mother...

                 (Sound: a blast of wind.

                 Light shift. LEVICK crawls into view, sifting snow in a stuporous panic.)

LEVICK: *(To God.)* We'll lose track of the days!

                 (Sound: more wind. a peel of boyish laughter.

                 LEVICK looks up, stunned. A smile.)

BOY'S VOICE: *(Off, distant.)* Daddy, come get me!

                 (LEVICK's expression falters under the weight of memory. DICKASON appears, pauses to watch.)

LEVICK: *(To the heavens.)* Stephen?

                 (LEVICK's face contorts. DICKASON is transfixed.)

DICKASON: Lose something, sir?

LEVICK: Lose? Yes. Afraid so.

                 (LEVICK digs at the snow.)

Utterly hopeless, I'm afraid. I'd prefer that you didn't mention this little mishap to the others.

DICKASON: Less said, soonest mended, sir. *(Pause.)* What did you lose?

LEVICK: The days. Without a chronometer how will we keep track?

DICKASON: *(Alarm.)* The chronometer, sir?

LEVICK: The lanyard looked as if it'd been cut with a knife. One wonders how such an accident could occur.

> *(They crawl off, searching in a panic.*
>
> *Sound: wind.*
>
> *Light cross-fade: to favour the snow cave.)*

BROWNING: *(Sobbing.)* —and she opened the oven door to show me and there I saw a human form trussed on a spit, the skin lifting back in black curls like the crackling on a pig, and I knew it to be the body of my father.

CAMPBELL: A nightmare, Browning. Nothing more.

BROWNING: Something has been released within me, sir. I cannot control it!

CAMPBELL: You must, Browning. You will.

BROWNING: I should croak and be done with it, sir.

CAMPBELL: *(Sharp.)* Don't talk nonsense.

BROWNING: The toes of my left foot, sir. They have all turned black.

PRIESTLEY: When?

BROWNING: For some weeks, sir. I can't take off my finnescoe for the smell.

CAMPBELL: *(To PRIESTLEY.)* Lets have a look.

> *(PRIESTLEY sets about unwrapping BROWN-ING's foot. ABBOTT watches carefully.)*

PRIESTLEY: Calm down, Browning.

BROWNING: *(Sobbing.)* I can't!

CAMPBELL: You must!

BROWNING: *(Blind panic.)* Don't you see? The ship picked up the Pole Party and foundered with all hands. We are the only survivors! Even if help is sent no one will ever think of looking for us on this shore! We'll watch each other die one by one and I shall be the first!

> *(PRIESTLEY uncovers BROWNING's black and swollen foot. BROWNING gasps in terror.)*

CAMPBELL: *(Gently.)* Patience, Charlie.

ABBOTT: Jumping Jesus.

CAMPBELL: I will thank you to keep your peace!

> *(CAMPBELL looks at the horrible foot. The worst has come to pass.)*

Why on earth didn't you tell us?

BROWNING: I was afraid to, sir. I'd be letting down the side.

> *(LEVICK enters via the tunnel. Takes in the scene at a glance, moves to examine the rotting foot.)*

LEVICK: No cause for alarm. Dab some zinc ointment on the open bits. Keep it dry. Good as new in no time.

BROWNING: I won't be losing my toes, sir?

LEVICK: Depends where the margin forms. I think we'll manage to save all five little piggies.

BROWNING: Oh thank you, Mother, thank you.

> *(DICKASON enters through the tunnel.)*

CAMPBELL: Let this be a caution to us all. We share a common body here. This damaged foot is attached to everyone. In future we must nip all such health problems in the bud. To do otherwise is an act of blatant irresponsibility. I could write this up on your flimsy, Rings. It's not the sort of thing a man wants on his record.

BROWNING: Very sorry, sir.

CAMPBELL: We will all learn from this. Be still now. Focus your energies on healing.

BROWNING: My foot, sir, could we cover it? The stench—

CAMPBELL: Abbott—

(ABBOTT moves to wrap the blackened foot back in its finniscoe.)

PRIESTLEY: I'd like to distribute sugars, sir.

CAMPBELL: Fine idea. It will lift our spirits. *(To DICKASON.)* Sing for us, Dickie. "Absent Friends".

(PRIESTLEY distributes sugar cubes. A kind of communion.)

DICKASON: *(Singing.)* Eternal father, strong to save / Whose arm doth bind the restless wave /

(ABBOTT sings to BROWNING, encouraging him to fight on. The magic works.)

ABBOTT &
DICKASON: Who bidd'st the mighty ocean deep / Its own appointed limits keep / O hear us when we cry to Thee / For those in peril on the sea.

ALL: O Saviour, whose almighty word / The winds and waves submissive heard / Who walkedst on the foaming deep / And calm amidst its rage didst sleep / O hear us when we cry to Thee / For those in peril on the sea.

(Sound: wind up.

Light shift:

ABBOTT and DICKASON converse in whispers.)

ABBOTT: Have you noticed anything?

DICKASON: What?

ABBOTT: About Number One.

DICKASON: What?

ABBOTT: He's lost track of the days.

DICKASON: What are you talking about?

ABBOTT: He's giving out sugars on a Saturday.

DICKASON: Yesterday was Saturday. This is Sunday.

ABBOTT: No. He's got it wrong.

(ABBOTT flashes the chronometer.)

It's Saturday.

DICKASON: You've no business with that.

ABBOTT: Somebody has to know what day it is.

DICKASON: I want no part of this.

ABBOTT: I've told Browning. He's in league with us.

DICKASON: What do you mean?

ABBOTT: What was, isn't. We're fighting for our lives. We need you with us.

(ABBOTT forces the chronometer into his hands.)

I'm putting you in charge of the days, Dog.

(ABBOTT moves back toward his bag.)

DICKASON: What do you expect of me?

ABBOTT: I've no plan. Haven't you had enough of plans?

DICKASON: But, what—

ABBOTT: We own the days. We stand together. There's no other way.

(DICKASON is flummoxed.)

Blind obedience is a form of madness. Be not afraid, Dog. I won't let you slip into madness.

(DICKASON sinks down into his bag. ABBOTT stares into the audience.

Light: snap to black.

Sound: wind up and out.

Sound: tink-a-tink-a-tink-a-tink.

LIGHTS UP ON: The cave. The men are eating hoosh in their bags. LEVICK, CAMPBELL and PRIESTLEY eat like proper gentlemen. The Men have atrocious eating habits. DICKASON sneezes in his bowl and licks it clean like a dog. ABBOTT makes his scraping sound...a steady rhythm. BROWNING unconsciously picks up the beat. Then DICKASON joins in. A rudimentary rhythm band.)

CAMPBELL: Enough.

(They stop the noise.

Sound: wind burst on roof.)

CAMPBELL: *(Awe.)* That's a seventy knot wind.

ABBOTT: What time is it, sir?

CAMPBELL: Seventeen-hundred hours.

(DICKASON and BROWNING exchange a glance. DICKASON reaches in his pocket. ABBOTT glares at him.

Sound: wind burst on roof.)

BROWNING: Listen to it—

(Sound: bigger wind.)

PRIESTLEY: Good Lord—

ABBOTT: The demons are upon us, boys.

BROWNING: *(Tiny.)* Doom.

(LEVICK eats a biscuit. Cool as a cucumber.)

CAMPBELL: Remain calm. The roof will hold.

(A nervous pause. ABBOTT smokes.)

BROWNING: How much tobacco have you left, Tiny?

ABBOTT: This isn't tickler. It's wood shavings.

BROWNING: Pleasant effect?

ABBOTT: Gets the job done.

BROWNING: Lets have a woof.

> *(BROWNING takes a drag.)*

Subtle. Very nice in the aftertaste.

CAMPBELL: Where did you get the wood shavings?

ABBOTT: I carved them off one of the packing crates on the sledge. Sir.

CAMPBELL: You *what?*

ABBOTT: I took some shavings off a specimen case.

> *(Sound: wind burst.)*

CAMPBELL: We can't be breaching crates to satisfy your addictions, Abbott.

ABBOTT: I just curled a little wood off with me pen knife.

CAMPBELL: I have made myself clear.

ABBOTT: As you say. Sir.

CAMPBELL: Further, I'd like to institute a new rule. No smoking in the cave until all have finished dinner.

ABBOTT: *(Extinguishing his fag.)* Right you are.

CAMPBELL: We are not animals. We will not live like animals.

> *(Sound: massive wind.)*

ABBOTT: *(Smile, whisper.)* The beast is hungry.

> *(DICKASON is holding his hand out to CAMPBELL. CAMPBELL doesn't notice. He's up on his knees, listening hard. LEVICK is concerned.)*

LEVICK: *(Covering.)* Shall we have a look at my cache of raisins?

(The spell is broken. CAMPBELL comes back to himself.)

CAMPBELL: Of course—

(All eyes on LEVICK as he unwraps a filthy rag.)

LEVICK: Hello lovelies…

BROWNING: *(To ABBOTT.)* Da-ding. Da-ding. The door to The South Pole is always open. I sit by the fire and tell my stories. Mother and the cache of raisins…

LEVICK: *(To CAMPBELL.)* A king's ransom in muscatels.

ABBOTT: Are you going to eat one tonight, Mother?

LEVICK: Just sightseeing for the moment.

DICKASON: Muscatel. Sometimes I say the word over and over to make me mouth water.

ABBOTT: *(Sexual.)* Jam 'em all in. I dare you.

(LEVICK opens his mouth, bends to the raisins, playing a game.)

ABBOTT: Oh yes…

CAMPBELL: Mother is merely setting a standard for self-control and a fine example it is. What are we up to now, Mother?

LEVICK: Sixty-three.

DICKASON: Sixty-three!

LEVICK: Ohhhh the heft of them.

BROWNING: Eat one.

(LEVICK savours his cache one final time.)

LEVICK: I don't think so. Not tonight. Perhaps tomorrow. Maybe I'll save them until Midwinter's Eve. What a feast that would be!

PRIESTLEY: June 21st. That's a long haul from here.

(He repackages them.)

BROWNING: There's a lot to be said for hoarding rations the way you do.

LEVICK: A little mound of time.

PRIESTLEY: Yes! *(Writes in his journal.)*

BROWNING: Gentlemen, it is official. I'm hoarding sugars.

(Sound: massive wind burst.

CAMPBELL focuses on the roof. Listening.)

CAMPBELL: Did you hear that? A voice—

LEVICK: A hurricane, sir.

DICKASON: *(Prayer.)* Muscatel. Muscatel. Muscatel.

LEVICK: *(Covering.)* Shall we begin our lecture series to-night? *(Showing the book.)* Breasted's *History of Egypt.* The volume has been a wonderful companion on this expedition and, having read it three times, I thought I might exercise my understanding of the text.

CAMPBELL: Ancient Egypt. Jolly good.

PRIESTLEY: To the land of the pharaohs!

LEVICK: First, we of the Modern Age must adjust the mind's eye, for we are going thousands of years back in time...

DICKASON: Oh my.

BROWNING: This is good, I like this.

LEVICK: The roots of modern civilization are planted deep in the basin of the eastern Mediterranean.

ABBOTT: Beirut. Have you ever been to Beirut? Beautiful girls. Smell like cloves, they do. A week later you wake up with Black Dong and the Doo-lally Tap.

(Laughter.)

BROWNING: When was you there, Tiny?

ABBOTT: I been a lot of places.

              (Laughter.)

CAMPBELL: Gentlemen—

LEVICK: I think our confinement has taught us how power-
              fully the forces of nature can react upon the mind
              and so it was for the ancient Egyptian.

              *(ABBOTT drones appropriate snake charmer
              music. Mimes a cobra with his hand.)*

BROWNING: *(Calling to prayers.)* Allaaaaah! Allaaaah Akhbar!

              (Laughter.)

LEVICK: There is no Allah yet. The Prophet Mohammed
              won't be born for three thousand years.

              (Sound: massive wind.)

CAMPBELL: Who was their god?

LEVICK: They had many deities, chiefly Ra, the sun god.
              Examine your own feelings about the sun here in
              our desert kingdom. At the dawn of civilization
              man had a different relationship with nature. The
              course of the sun in the sky. The shape of a cloud
              over the ocean. A wind. Everything carried a
              message from beyond. Man behaved like a child
              who believes the world is created solely for him.
              God was whispering in his ear all day long.
              (Whisper.) They rolled the day forward like a great
              boulder. Priests wearing jackal heads moving in
              the shadows...the rustle of their garments...

              (LEVICK pauses to check his audience.)

              Still with me, Tiny?

DICKASON: Who was it come up with the idea for the
              pyramids?

LEVICK: You speak of the great pyramids opposite modern
              day Cairo?

DICKASON: The ones on the syrup bottle.

LEVICK: Gizeh, built by the Pharaoh Khufu some three thousand years before the birth of Christ. Herodotus relates a traditional story that this tomb demanded the labour of a hundred thousand men for twenty years.

All of this happening before Britain entered the Bronze Age.

ABBOTT: Why?

LEVICK: What do you mean?

ABBOTT: Why did they bother?

LEVICK: The final key to eternal life was to perpetuate your name and have it spoken by the living. That's what this is all about.

ABBOTT: That's fine for the bloke in the tomb. What about the lad who spent his life going at the rock with a hammer and chisel?

CAMPBELL: He was a happy man.

ABBOTT: Why?

CAMPBELL: In my experience men are happiest when they are dwarfed by their projects.

ABBOTT: These weren't 'men'. They were slaves.

LEVICK: *Words.* Words were a potent form of magic for the ancient Egyptian. The chiselled inscriptions on the tombs state plainly that these buildings were intended to stand forever. I would put it to you that the man with the chisel felt the power of the words he was inscribing. They caused events to occur. In his own small way he was conquering time.

(Sound: wind. CAMPBELL listens hard.)

PRIESTLEY: *(Writing in his journal.)* I chisel, therefore I am.

LEVICK: Precisely.

CAMPBELL: And so we write in our journals, or name a head-
             land after a notable from home, hoping the world
             will remember our passing.

ABBOTT: *(Sneer.)* Nobody will remember us.

             *(ABBOTT looks into CAMPBELL's eyes. Others
             feel the tension.)*

BROWNING: Maybe they'll read Dickason's journal. Every entry
             starts: Cold, windy.

DICKASON: True, isn't it?

             (Small laughter.)

LEVICK: All gone now, thousands of years of human his-
             tory. All that remains are these titanic monuments
             with their frail inscriptions.

CAMPBELL: The Priestley Glacier! Mount Browning! Cape
             Dickason! Don't smile. We're surrounded by fea-
             tures that need names. Those who pull with me
             will be remembered. I intend to set my mind to the
             matter very shortly.

DICKASON: I'd like a snug anchorage named after me, sir. That
             way I'd always be part of a certain kind of story.
             "Finally we made it to Dickason Cove, and our
             lives were saved."

BROWNING: I want to be part of a grand panorama. "We stood
             atop Mount Browning and saw a hundred miles."

ABBOTT: "He fell down a crevasse on the Abbott Ice Tongue
             and was never heard from again."

             (Nervous laughter.)

PRIESTLEY: We must name this place where we are marooned.

CAMPBELL: Impossible. These living conditions are beyond
             description.

             (Sound: massive wind.)

PRIESTLEY: *(To LEVICK.)* Inexpressible Island.

LEVICK: Jolly good! *(To CAMPBELL.)* Inexpressible Island.
               What do you think?

CAMPBELL: *(Disdain.)* It has a rather *modern* ring. I'll take the
               matter under advisement.

               (The space falls quiet.)

BROWNING: A thousand years from now they'll stand in Trafal-
               gar Square, look up at Nelson's column and think,
               what? What will they think?

CAMPBELL: They'll think, the English, a great civilization, a
               seafaring nation and there stands her greatest na-
               val commander.

ABBOTT: That's not what they'll think.

CAMPBELL: Tell us what they'll think, Abbott.

               (Everyone waits.)

ABBOTT: They'll think, I wonder if I can shinny up there and
               chop off that swanky's noggin.

               (Laughter.)

LEVICK: And so we steal from ourselves. Vandalize
               memory, break off our connections with the past,
               leaving behind more than we carry forward. One
               often feels that mankind has forgotten more than it
               knows.

               (Sound: wind on the roof.

               CAMPBELL mutters.)

CAMPBELL: *(To ABBOTT.)* We think we know so much.

ABBOTT: We know nothing.

               (Sound: a more powerful gust.)

CAMPBELL: Time for the evening anemometer reading. Where
               are we in the rotation?

BROWNING: My go, sir.

               (BROWNING starts to pull on his boots.)

CAMPBELL: Up, up, up. That's the stuff.

LEVICK: No! I'm sorry, sir. Browning is confined to quarters until we see some improvement in that foot.

> *(LEVICK has cut across CAMPBELL's command. A nervous pause. No volunteers. CAMPBELL reaches for his boots.)*

CAMPBELL: Very well.

> *(Sound: more wind.)*

DICKASON: No man should be out in that.

CAMPBELL: We have a plan! We will stick to it!

> *(CAMPBELL prepares to exit; he's in a fury. A sense of unease from BROWNING, DICKASON and LEVICK. ABBOTT is fascinated.)*

LEVICK: Sir—

CAMPBELL: A plan! Does anyone else here have a plan?

> *(Nervous eye contact.)*

DICKASON: *(To LEVICK.)* Interesting talk, sir.

LEVICK: You see how it goes. One thing to the next.

PRIESTLEY: A fire to warm the hands.

CAMPBELL: We inhabit an historical moment, gentlemen. Our undertaking here matches *anything* from the ancient world! I'd like to see you all writing in your journals. If you will excuse me, I have an appointment with the wind.

DICKASON: It's blowing a hurricane, sir.

CAMPBELL: Good.

> *(CAMPBELL makes his exit.*
>
> *Sound: wind builds.*
>
> *LEVICK doesn't know what to do now. Real alarm from DICKASON and BROWNING.)*

BROWNING: I am so afraid. Please, Mother. Do something.

LEVICK: (*Desperation.*) I—I could…I could recite a poem.

DICKASON: Please…

            (*ABBOTT points at the ceiling and makes his sizzling sound.*)

LEVICK: Come along, Tiny. Join the group.

ABBOTT: A poem. Jolly good.

LEVICK: (*Holding emotion.*) "In Xanadu did Kubla Khan / A stately pleasure dome decree / Where Alph, the sacred river, ran / Through caverns measureless to man / Down to a sunless sea…"

            (*To black. Hurricane winds.*)

            Single spot on whirling anemometer. High above.

            Light shift. CAMPBELL appears, leaning into the ferocious gale, following a guide rope toward the wind gauge. The wind tears at him.)

CAMPBELL: Raise the bar! I command it! We have our training! Up, up, up, up, UP! Mind over matter!

            (*Sound: massive wind burst.*

            CAMPBELL leans into the wind, his face a foot from the ground.)

            Pull with me…and be remembered!

            (*Sound: wind burst.*

            CAMPBELL falls to his knees and crabs forward into the gale.)

            (*A grail.*) Drake! Raleigh! Cook!

            (*CAMPBELL exits. The rope stretches taut behind him and undulates like a sonic wave.*)

CAMPBELL: (*Off.*) CAMPBELL!

ECHO: Campbell!

CAMPBELL: *(Off.)* CAMPBELL!

ECHO: Campbell!

> *(The rope breaks free and arcs high overhead.*
>
> *Light shift: to favour the cave.*
>
> *ABBOTT kneels before Dr. LEVICK, mouth wide open. An act of primitive supplication. LEVICK probes inside ABBOTT's mouth with a surgical instrument. DICKASON is restless, a dog without his master.*
>
> *Sound: wind burst.)*

DICKASON: Did you hear something?

PRIESTLEY: What?

DICKASON: Number One. I thought I heard him calling.

BROWNING: The wind. I'm always hearing me mum.

LEVICK: *(To ABBOTT.)* Steady. Steady.

BROWNING: Is it possible for wind to drive a man mad, Mother?

> *(LEVICK makes a quick stabbing movement. ABBOTT gags and sputters with pain. Spits a gout of blood and pus into his handkerchief.)*

LEVICK: Put some ice on it.

> *(ABBOTT returns to his place.)*

Your question?

BROWNING: Is it possible for the wind to drive a man insane?

LEVICK: Anemomania. That's the medical term for it. Wind madness.

DICKASON: *(Warding off evil.)* Muscatel. Muscatel. Muscatel.

BROWNING: I heard that when men die of cold they've been found absolutely stripped with their clothes lying all about them on the ice, as if their last sensation had been of intolerable heat.

ABBOTT: Heat and cold meet.

BROWNING: Like tears and laughter.

LEVICK: Lovely, Rings.

BROWNING: Why thank you, Mother.

PRIESTLEY: *(To LEVICK.)* Perhaps we should go and give Lieutenant Campbell a hand.

LEVICK: *(Very calm.)* Indeed.

DICKASON: I could help with that, sir.

LEVICK: No cause for alarm. Finish preparing the hoosh.

                (PRIESTLEY and LEVICK exit the cave in haste.

                Pause.)

ABBOTT: Ahhh, it's turning now. Poor Campbell, outside crying in the wind. *(To DICKASON.)* You were going to betray us!

DICKASON: You've got no plan. At least he has a plan.

                (ABBOTT laughs at that.)

ABBOTT: I'll show you a fucking plan. *(Pointing.)* My crack! Look at it! Every day, a little longer, a little wider.

BROWNING: Which one?

ABBOTT: The big one, donkey. *My* crack!

BROWNING: Why is it yours?

ABBOTT: I make it bigger. Inch by inch.

DICKASON: How?

ABBOTT: I can heat things up with my eyes.

BROWNING: Bollocks.

ABBOTT: Believe what you like.

BROWNING: Let's feel this heat. Look at me.

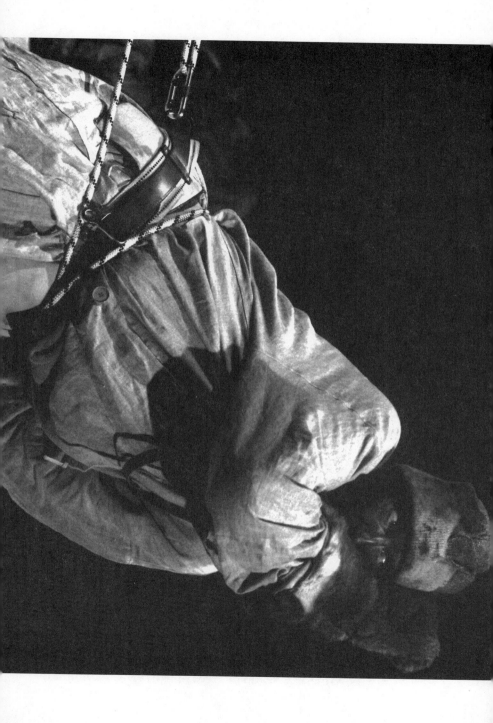

(ABBOTT and BROWNING turn to face each other. Pause.)

BROWNING: *(cont'd)* That does feel rather warmish.

(DICKASON is leaning into ABBOTT's eye-line, curious.)

ABBOTT: Bad dog. You get none of my heat.

DICKASON: Don't listen to him. He's lost his mind.

ABBOTT: Ho-ho. Have I?

(ABBOTT sits up, reaches over to rummage under CAMPBELL's bag.)

You're the one who is lost, Dog. Following your master no matter what. You should read what he says about you—

(ABBOTT leafs through CAMPBELL's journal. BROWNING and DICKASON are aghast.)

DICKASON: You've no right to—

ABBOTT: Dog can't know his master's private thoughts? The whole system might explode? Here it is! *(Reading.)* "A child in a man's body, happy only when he is treated as a child...incapable of making the simplest decisions without my approval—"

BROWNING: Don't listen.

ABBOTT: *(Reading.)* "Reminds me of a dray horse I rode as a lad in Durham." Interesting stuff.

(ABBOTT flips the journal into DICKASON's hands. At that moment PRIESTLEY and LEVICK drag CAMPBELL into the tunnel. He has been shattered by the cold.)

PRIESTLEY: Make way! Make way!

CAMPBELL: *(Thick stupor.)* Bone-cutting wind. Eighty knots with forty-seven degrees of frost. The anemometer was listing badly so I resecured it. Safety lines in top nick.

LEVICK: Get in my bag.

CAMPBELL: I shall be just fine.

LEVICK: Get in my bag!

CAMPBELL: Has Mr. Priestley distributed the biscuits? *(Shaking DICKASON.)* Rise and shine, Mr. Priestley. I've been thinking about my biscuit all morning. I can't feel my face.

> *(CAMPBELL falls into LEVICK's bag. His whole body is chattering.)*

May we have our biscuit, please!

> *(PRIESTLEY produces the lid. A sense that they hang on the cusp of catastrophe. The biscuit ritual is the last thread. DICKASON quietly pushes the chronometer into CAMPBELL's hands. CAMPBELL is stunned. ABBOTT gives DICKASON a look of pure hatred.)*

PRIESTLEY: Rings?

> *(BROWNING covers his eyes.)*

Whose is this?

BROWNING: Lieutenant Campbell.

> *(PRIESTLEY distributes the biscuits.)*

PRIESTLEY: And this?

BROWNING: Dr. Levick.

PRIESTLEY: Next?

BROWNING: You, sir.

PRIESTLEY: How about this little rotter?

BROWNING: Dickason.

PRIESTLEY: And again?

BROWNING: That's mine, sir.

(PRIESTLEY hands the last one to ABBOTT.)

ABBOTT: It's in six fucking pieces.

LEVICK: The luck of the draw.

ABBOTT: In a pig's eye.

(CAMPBELL rises up on one elbow.)

CAMPBELL: Is—is there a problem, Abbott?

ABBOTT: It's always the same. Browning goes down through the ranks. The last biscuit is the worst biscuit and it always lands in the stokehold.

CAMPBELL: Heaven forbid that we should be unfair to the stokehold, Abbott. Everyone return your biscuits to Mr. Priestley. I have another plan. A little game learned at my father's knee on the Royal yacht *Victoria & Albert*. Choose a word with more than six letters and write it down.

(LEVICK thinks, writes.)

LEVICK: Done.

CAMPBELL: How many letters?

LEVICK: Nine.

CAMPBELL: *(To ABBOTT.)* Select a number between one and nine. The first letter in Dr. Levick's word is number one.

LEVICK: I see how you're going. Jolly good.

ABBOTT: I don't.

CAMPBELL: Choose a number, one to nine.

ABBOTT: Five.

(CAMPBELL points to the others one by one. LEVICK notes their choices.)

BROWNING: Two.

DICKASON: One.

PRIESTLEY: Four.

CAMPBELL: I will take three. *(To LEVICK.)* And for you I will choose number six. What was the word?

LEVICK: Facetious.

ABBOTT: Never heard of it.

CAMPBELL: I thought you were being facetious, Abbott. I thought you were joking. Dr. Levick, who goes first?

LEVICK: Browning, then you, sir—

(They choose their biscuits in order.)

LEVICK: Mr. Priestley. Dickason, me...and bringing up the rear—

(ABBOTT picks up the six pieces of biscuit. He can't believe it.)

ABBOTT: That was very clever, whatever the fuck it was.

CAMPBELL: Abbott, I would prefer it if you curbed your colourful language when we are in company. When you are on the other side of the invisible wall you may speak like a pimp at a whore's tea party. When we are here together I would appreciate a measure of decorum.

ABBOTT: I have a question about the invisible wall, sir.

CAMPBELL: I'm listening.

ABBOTT: How do we know if it's up or down?

CAMPBELL: I would have thought that would be self-evident.

ABBOTT: I'm afraid it's not. There are times that I'm surprised to be overheard. I think the wall is up, and it's not.

DICKASON: Tiny is a bit thick.

CAMPBELL: Easy enough to sort out. Come up with a signal, Tiny.

(ABBOTT sticks his knife in the floor.)

ABBOTT: That means the wall is up.

CAMPBELL: Careful. You don't want to cut yourself under these conditions. You've got a large discharging abscess in your mouth.

ABBOTT: It's nice behind the invisible wall. You can't hear a fucking thing.

(ABBOTT lights a cigarette, lies back in his bag. CAMPBELL is staring at his knife.)

(To BROWNING.) Who was the worst commander you ever had.

BROWNING: Well, let me think, I'm not sure…

CAMPBELL: Dickason.

DICKASON: Yes sir.

CAMPBELL: Do a daily check on all the crates on the sledge. Report any damage or deterioration to me immediately.

ABBOTT: Come on then. The very worst. The lowest of the low.

DICKASON: As you say, sir.

CAMPBELL: Browning.

(Pause. ABBOTT holds BROWNING's gaze.)

Browning.

(Another pause. ABBOTT smiles.)

BROWNING: Yes sir.

CAMPBELL: You are confined to quarters until we see some improvement in that foot.

BROWNING: I want to pull my weight, sir.

CAMPBELL: There will be ample opportunity for contribution. You can help me clean this filthy midden tomorrow morning.

BROWNING: Aye aye, sir.

CAMPBELL: Abbott.

(ABBOTT smokes.)

Abbott.

(ABBOTT smokes.)

ABBOTT!

ABBOTT: The wind. I think I hear me father.

CAMPBELL: *(Pointing at the knife.)* Where did you get that lanyard?

ABBOTT: Found a bit of cord lying around.

CAMPBELL: I don't think that's what happened at all.

(CAMPBELL compares ABBOTT's knife lanyard to his chronometer lanyard. A perfect match.)

You, my good man, are a sneak. A sneak, Abbott! A FILTHY LYING SNEAK!

(ABBOTT smokes, stares at the ceiling.)

LOOK AT ME WHEN I ADDRESS YOU!

(ABBOTT smokes, points at his crack, makes a sizzling sound.)

BASTARD! OUTSIDE! INTO THE WIND!

(CAMPBELL is suddenly terrifyingly focused. He has ABBOTT's knife in his hand.)

MOVE! NOW!

LEVICK: Sir!

(ABBOTT butts his cigarette. Smirks.)

ABBOTT: Here's where we are, lads. Look at it. I'm not afraid of the fucking wind. *(To BROWNING and DICKASON.)* "Let your hearts not be troubled. I go to prepare a place for you."

(ABBOTT backs out of the cave, laughing as he goes. There is a long, terrible pause.)

LEVICK: It's blowing a hurricane, sir.

CAMPBELL: Good. *(To the men.)* Go to sleep!

(CAMPBELL disappears into his bag. LEVICK searches for a way to release the tension.)

LEVICK: *(To BROWNING.)* Are you going to feast in your dreams tonight?

BROWNING: I—I hope so, Mother.

CAMPBELL: *(From his bag.)* Go to the castle. The father and his three fucking sons. Eat like a gannet!

BROWNING: *(Morose.)* As you say, sir.

(They settle in their bags.

Sound: a horrendous wash of wind.

Light: Levels dim to favour LEVICK and PRIESTLEY. They speak in low tones.)

PRIESTLEY: *(Whisper.)* What will happen to him?

LEVICK: *(Whisper.)* He is in God's hands.

PRIESTLEY: *(Suddenly overcome.)* Please…please…

LEVICK: It is beyond our control.

(Pause.)

PRIESTLEY: *(Unstrung.)* I want to go home.

LEVICK: Shh. It's alright. I'll take you there. Get on.

(PRIESTLEY clings to LEVICK.)

PRIESTLEY: An evening journey, Mother. Country lanes.

LEVICK: I know a lovely cake shop in Devon. It's dusk, the first stars and planets pinned along the horizon. Crickets. I kick us into low gear. Coast down a long drive lined with beech trees. The rustle of their leaves.

(Light shift to reflect their imagining.)

LEVICK: A thin paring of moon.

PRIESTLEY: I want full moonlight.

LEVICK: Fine. Full moon it is. We accelerate beneath a bower of chestnut trees. Pavement stencilled with silver moonshadow. It's early October but the evening heat belongs more properly to mid-summer. One of those lovely surprises—

PRIESTLEY: The final pulse of the fading season.

LEVICK: Exactly so. "Here at the roaring loom of Time I ply / And weave for God the garment thou seest him by."

PRIESTLEY: Keats.

LEVICK: Yes, accelerating now, out of the tunnel of trees, into the vastness of the night...the grand sprawl of the heavens...

(Light shift: PRIESTLEY comes to his feet.)

PRIESTLEY: May 21st, 1912. In the dream I awake and I am old.

(The tremble returns in increments.)

So very old. I creep out of the tunnel. The night is hard, clear. The stars, steel points, the glacier a river of burnished silver. The snow rings and thuds to my footfall. Ice moves. A roll of distant thunder. The still further cooling of the earth. Abbott? ABBOTT!

ECHO: Abbott.

(PRIESTLEY is alone in the last light.)

PRIESTLEY: *(Terror.)* A great silence descends from the heavens...a silence I can feel on my skin...

(Fade to black.

End of ACT TWO.)

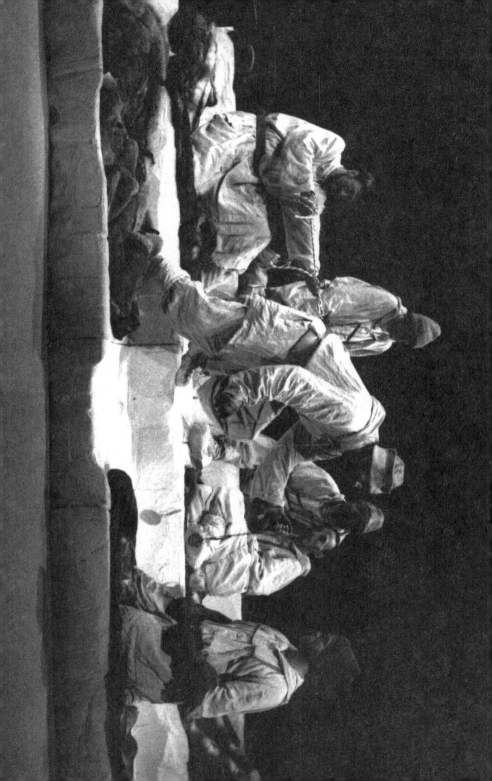

ACT THREE

(Music wash: Meredith Monk. Mad Whispers.

Sound: Enormous wind.

Lights up to low levels: ABBOTT kneels. A mad stare, his whole body juddering. He fights to stand in the wind, fails. The cold tears at him.

Sound: katabatic burst.

The wind knocks him flat.

Snap light shift: single on PRIESTLEY: He sits bolt upright in his chair, awakened by the nightmare. Trembles with memory.

Light cross-fades to: flickering fire. As the nightmare fades.

DICKASON enters.)

PRIESTLEY: Dozed off, one foot in dream.

DICKASON: Did you find the entry you were looking for, sir?

PRIESTLEY: *(Reading.)* May 22, 1912. The seventy-first day of our confinement. Black as a coal sack with a hundred and seven degrees of frost. Campbell cross with Abbott. Browning's foot in deplorable condition. I cannot remember the name of the pet turtle I kept as a child and am greatly troubled by it...end of journal entry. *(Pause.)* My pet turtle!—and not a word about Dr. Levick's intercession.

DICKASON: Was Mother who saved us that day.

PRIESTLEY: It was Abbott.

DICKASON: I think you got him wrong, sir. He was pulling at us from below.

PRIESTLEY: Precisely. Down-down-down…to Time Zero.

               (Light shift: To reveal a tableau: LEVICK examines the bottom of BROWNING's blackened foot. CAMPBELL holds the lamp. No movement. Pieces of the ice cave are set about them like Easter Island monoliths.)

DICKASON: Sir?

PRIESTLEY: There was something released in that cave, Dickie. Its shadow is still upon us…

               (Sound up: air raid siren from the Blitz.)

DICKASON: We must dim the lights.

               (DICKASON does so. Pause. The siren moans. PRIESTLEY struggles for control.)

DICKASON: Are you alright, sir?

PRIESTLEY: No. I am not.

               (PRIESTLEY could cry, but he doesn't. He leads DICKASON into the tableau.)

PRIESTLEY: Do you ever think about the mountain Lieutenant Campbell named after you, Dickie?

DICKASON: *(Hostile edge.)* Never a thought, sir.

               (Sound: air raid siren fades out.

               PRIESTLEY and DICKASON sit into the tableau, triggering small movements from LEVICK and CAMPBELL.)

BROWNING: *(Distracting himself.)* Da-ding. Da-ding. The door to the South Pole is always open. It will be such a fine tea shop, Dickie.

LEVICK: Feel that?

BROWNING: No.

LEVICK: That?

BROWNING: I feel nothing, sir.

LEVICK: Good. Light, please.

> *(CAMPBELL moves the light closer.)*

> *(To PRIESTLEY.)* Use the tweezers to hold that bit back.

> *(PRIESTLEY does as he's told.)*

BROWNING: I've got a hungry beast inside me. I feel it scraping my ribs.

LEVICK: Be still.

BROWNING: *(To DICKASON.)* Talk to me. Tell me something. Anything.

LEVICK: *(Sotto, to CAMPBELL.)* How long has he been out?

CAMPBELL: *(Checks chronometer.)* Six hours.

DICKASON: *(In BROWNING's ear.)* "Here at the roaring loom of Time, I ply / And weave for God the garment thou seest Him by."

BROWNING: What's that?

DICKASON: Lines from a poem. I heard someone say them. Stuck in my ear.

PRIESTLEY: Keats.

LEVICK: He could die.

CAMPBELL: He has a lesson to learn.

BROWNING: What's it mean?

DICKASON: How would I know? It's a poem.

> *(LEVICK, calm and concentrated, lifts a slab of skin away from the sole of BROWNING's foot.)*

BROWNING: *(Laughing.)* You've lost your mind, Dog.

LEVICK: How long will his banishment last?

CAMPBELL: *(Twitch smile.)* Depends entirely on the man. For-
             ever, if need be.

LEVICK: You must set a limit.

CAMPBELL: Oh, *must* I?

LEVICK: A task. Something.

             *(LEVICK has finished with BROWNING's foot. He
             rebandages it.)*

             Coming along quite nicely.

BROWNING: Thank you, Mother.

             *(DICKASON examines the dead flesh from
             BROWNING's foot.)*

CAMPBELL: He must kill us a seal.

BROWNING: What is that?

DICKASON: The sole of your foot.

BROWNING: That's my sole?

LEVICK: The body has marvellous powers of regeneration.

BROWNING: I've lost my sole?

             (BROWNING begins to laugh and cry.)

             Give it back, sir! Please.

CAMPBELL: *(To LEVICK.)* Put it back on.

LEVICK: *(Unwrapping BROWNING's foot.)* If it makes you
             feel better. *(To CAMPBELL.)* Someone must take
             word to him.

CAMPBELL: Mr. Priestley, go to Abbott. Tell him he will be
             welcome again in these quarters after he kills us a
             seal.

PRIESTLEY: I—I can't, sir.

CAMPBELL: Excuse me?

PRIESTLEY: I—I'm afraid of him.

CAMPBELL: Gunroom discipline, Mr. Priestley. Move!

(PRIESTLEY is frozen in place, horrified. He begins to tremble.)

BROWNING: *(Private, to LEVICK.)* Will it grow back on?

LEVICK: Of course.

(To black.

Sound: hurricane wind.

Light shift: A huddled figure moves backwards into the light, trying to protect himself from the hurricane. LEVICK reveals himself. He spots ABBOTT, goes to him and shakes him hard. No response.)

LEVICK: Nooo!

(ABBOTT sits up. He is in a hypothermic stupor.)

ABBOTT: *(Whisper.)* Fuck me. Fuck me. Fuck me.

LEVICK: God rest your soul.

(Sound: the wind subsides.)

ABBOTT: I need no help from the likes of you. Fucked up, far from home and happy with it.

LEVICK: You must kill a seal. Lieutenant Campbell commands it.

ABBOTT: *(Laughs.)* One final test. And if I don't?

LEVICK: You will die in darkness on the shore of this frozen sea.

ABBOTT: I will not die for you.

(ABBOTT falls on his side.)

LEVICK: I—I feel a special responsibility for you, Abbott.

ABBOTT: What?

LEVICK: Your stubborn streak.

(ABBOTT chortles.)

LEVICK: *(cont'd)* My son was like that.

ABBOTT: Didn't know you had a son, gov'nor.

LEVICK: Nobody in this party does. Stephen. My little boy didn't like to be told where he could and could not go. He was about two and a half, just at that stage when you do your first real thinking. Our cottage overlooked a tidal flat. A little jetty where you could float a skiff at high water. Stephen loved to go down there and watch the minnows. Not alone mind you. Never alone.

               (LEVICK beams.)

               Stubborn as a mule.

               (ABBOTT listens hard.)

               It was the minnows, you see. He slipped away to visit the minnows. Two feet of water. Not too much. Just enough.

               (Pause. LEVICK struggles, kneels beside ABBOTT.)

               Don't reach for the minnows, Tiny. That's the only advice I can give you.

               (LEVICK warms his hand and touches ABBOTT's cheek.)

ABBOTT: I'll keep that in mind, doctor.

               (SFX: Weddell seal.)

               (Drawing his knife.) Dinner bell.

               (He crawls away.)

LEVICK: *(Singing.)* Eternal Father, strong to save / Whose arm doth bind the restless wave—

               (Sound: wind up.

               LEVICK must drop to all fours. He exits, crawling, howling his hymn.

Light shift: To favour CAMPBELL in his bag. He has become a Weddell seal. He throws back his head and mimes a croon.

Sound: Weddell seal.

ABBOTT appears, knife in his teeth, stalking low, unseen.

Sound: Weddell seal.

ABBOTT lunges. The seal struggles to escape, twists around to try and bite.)

ABBOTT: Bastard!

(For a moment there is fierce struggle. ABBOTT plunges his knife into the seal again and again.)

I'll eat your fucking brain!

(ABBOTT screams in pain and rolls away holding his hand aloft, howling with pain. In the confusion he has given himself a terrible cut.

Light: snap to black.

Lights up slowly.

CAMPBELL thrashes awake, horrified by his dream. Members of the party are scattered around the stage in their bags. Various snores.)

BROWNING: *(Off, in his sleep.)* Why, yes, of course, lots of trifle...pile it on.

(PRIESTLEY's head appears.)

CAMPBELL: How's it coming, Dickie?

DICKASON: Not enough for a proper hoosh.

CAMPBELL: How many flippers do we have?

DICKASON: Four.

BROWNING: *(Off.)* Oh indeed...*delicious.*

PRIESTLEY: Having one of his food dreams.

> *(BROWNING appears, stretches.)*

DICKASON: Good sleep?

BROWNING: Weaving in and out. Listening to you lot grousing the whole time. Hard to settle into a meal when you can hear your friends jeering outside the window.

> *(CAMPBELL rummages for his journal at the foot of his bag.)*

CAMPBELL: Did someone move my journal?

> *(Pause.)*

> It's wrong way 'round. And my pencil...where's my pencil?

LEVICK: Not there?

ABBOTT: *(Off.)* Help! Help me!

> *(DICKASON pulls ABBOTT into the cave. ABBOTT's hand runs with fresh blood.)*

LEVICK: Great God...

ABBOTT: Fucking crab-eater. The knife slipped while I was killing him. I can't move me finger.

CAMPBELL: You bagged him?

ABBOTT: Oh yes.

> *(Roaring cheer.)*

> He's out by the sea front with his head half off.

ALL: Bravo! / Well done! / Jolly good!

ABBOTT: I get the head!

CAMPBELL: Dickason, go and fetch it in.

> *(DICKASON exits. LEVICK works on ABBOTT's hand.)*

ABBOTT: I can't move it.

LEVICK: Frozen solid, I'm afraid. The tendons are severed.

ABBOTT: Lord fucking Jesus!

CAMPBELL: Mr. Abbott, blasphemy is entirely inappropriate
               when one is in need of the Lord's assistance, as you
               are at—

ABBOTT: I'm going to lose me fucking hand!

               *(CAMPBELL stares hard at ABBOTT. ABBOTT
               stares right back. Pure animal aggression. They
               could kill each other.)*

LEVICK: No!

               *(LEVICK reaches to block their line of sight with a
               palm. He makes as if to snatch up everything in
               their exchange in his hand, the way one catches a fly
               mid-air. It's all there inside his clenched fist.
               LEVICK holds out his hand to PRIESTLEY.)*

               Take this evil outside. Send it away on the wind.

               *(PRIESTLEY is at first dumbfounded, then he plays
               along, cupping his hands, as if he's carrying an
               errant firefly out of the house on a summer night.)*

               (Gentle, to ABBOTT.) Come, lie here. Put your hand
               against me and I will thaw it for you.

               *(They rearrange themselves. CAMPBELL comes
               back to himself.)*

CAMPBELL: We'll boil up the head tonight, Tiny. You shall have
               the brain.

ABBOTT: All to myself?

CAMPBELL: You've done us proud.

ABBOTT: Thank you, sir.

LEVICK: *(To CAMPBELL and ABBOTT.)* Much better.

               (The family unpleasantness is over.

               Lights fade.)

(ABBOTT is lying beside LEVICK. PRIESTLEY is on his knees.)

LEVICK: *(To ABBOTT.)* Let your arm go loose. That's it. That's it.

(ABBOTT groans with a mixture of comfort and pain. The last light is on PRIESTLEY, kneeling. He holds his cupped hands up into the wind. The tremble comes into his body.)

(Off.) Oh, that's cold.

ABBOTT: *(Off.)* The hand of death, sir.

LEVICK: *(Off.)* It's alright. It's alright. There we go. Ahhhh.

(Sound: wind burst.

PRIESTLEY opens his hands.

Lights cross-fade to favour DICKASON, dragging the dead seal. He spots PRIESTLEY.)

DICKASON: What are you doing there, sir?

PRIESTLEY: Nothing.

DICKASON: Abbott come back, with a seal. I thought he was a dead man.

PRIESTLEY: We are all dead men. A question of time.

DICKASON: Sir?

(PRIESTLEY's face collapses.)

PRIESTLEY: I cannot go on.

DICKASON: You must, sir. You will.

(PRIESTLEY cries quietly.)

PRIESTLEY: Talk to me.

DICKASON: Think of the future. Where you want to be when all of this is done.

(PRIESTLEY regains himself in increments.)

PRIESTLEY: Back in England? No idea, really. My father is Sec-
retary of the British Rainfall Association. He thinks
he might be able to find me a permanent posting in
the organization.

DICKASON: *(Jollying him.)* British Rainfall Association. Sounds
steady enough.

PRIESTLEY: Suitably anonymous. Until I establish myself as a
writer.

DICKASON: That's the big plan, is it? Come on then. Up, up, up.

(PRIESTLEY has recovered sufficiently to stand.)

PRIESTLEY: I shall begin with a great sprawling novel about
Antarctica.

DICKASON: The story of this expedition, sir?

PRIESTLEY: I shall remember your every utterance, Dickie.

DICKASON: Oopsie-do. Wish I'd known that.

(They laugh.)

PRIESTLEY: What about you? The future.

DICKASON: It's uncertain, sir.

PRIESTLEY: I suppose it all depends on Lieutenant Campbell.

DICKASON: Not entirely.

PRIESTLEY: Oh?

DICKASON: Sometimes I wonder what would happen if I left
his command.

PRIESTLEY: He'd be at sixes and sevens without you, Dickie,
that's sure.

DICKASON: Sometimes things are not entirely as they seem, sir.

*(Light shift. We are back in the Cambridge drawing
room under Blitz conditions. A fire pops and cracks
in the grate. PRIESTLEY trembles.)*

PRIESTLEY: But you must remember the day. Dragging that

PRIESTLEY: *(cont'd)* seal back to the cave after Abbott received his injury?

DICKASON: I remember fetching the seal, sir. I can't remember what we talked about.

PRIESTLEY: The general drift was that you were thinking of leaving the service of Lieutenant Campbell.

DICKASON: Oh.

(Pause.)

PRIESTLEY: Have you heard from him?

DICKASON: Nary a word.

PRIESTLEY: He has a game lodge somewhere in the colonies. Newfoundland, I believe.

DICKASON: Black Duck Cove. Arse end of nowhere. Good spot for him.

PRIESTLEY: Pity it ended like that, after everything you two had been through together.

DICKASON: He told me I should never have to worry. There would always be employment. I did my bit.

PRIESTLEY: I know you did.

DICKASON: It was all a lie. Handed me his chronometer as a keepsake and sailed off into the fog.

(Pause.)

PRIESTLEY: I suppose it's the whole system at fault.

DICKASON: As you say, sir.

(Pause.)

PRIESTLEY: I had plans too. None of it turned out as I thought.

DICKASON: It has not been a good century, has it, sir?

PRIESTLEY: Who could have predicted?

DICKASON: I look back and I see us on the ice and all that's happened since and I can hardly believe it.

PRIESTLEY: That man in the Antarctic named Dickason has be-
               come a character in a tall tale told to grandchildren.

DICKASON: Exactly so, sir.

PRIESTLEY: And so we move in time...

               (Sound: wind burst.)

               The story rages past our door. It howls like a gale. It
               inundates and exhausts us. *(Pause.)* It eludes us.
               We grow old and die. No generation lives long
               enough to hear its story told. Presto. Time's
               winged arrow through the heart of the human con-
               dition. We never discover ourselves. *(Pause.)* Or so
               goes my theorem...

DICKASON: It sounds a sad story, sir.

PRIESTLEY: Tragedy stares us in the face, Dickie. We avert our
               gaze and do as we must. And at the end of our
               labours...*what?* Dying is easy...the difficult part
               is...

               (Uncomfortable pause. PRIESTLEY trembles.)

               The South is so often in my thoughts. *(Pause.)* No
               one understands.

DICKASON: *(Consoling.)* The eternity they speak of in church,
               sir. We crossed over into the mire and suck of it.
               Men are not supposed to see what we saw.

PRIESTLEY: And all that we learned will be forgotten.

DICKASON: I hope not, sir. You'll write your book for posterity.

               (PRIESTLEY smiles at that idea.)

PRIESTLEY: I'll tell you a little story about posterity. This past
               autumn Dr. Levick went to see his Emperor Pen-
               guin eggs at the British Museum.

DICKASON: *(Amused.)* Oh my!

PRIESTLEY: Tottered in expecting to find them on display or at
               least available for study and, of course, nobody
               knows ANYTHING about it. Emperor Penguin
               eggs? Never heard of 'em!

DICKASON: *(Laughing.)* I can see his face!

PRIESTLEY: Mother spent a day digging through the records.
               Deep in the bowels of the British Museum he opens
               this crate and…there they are…

               (DICKASON is ready for a snappy punch line.)

               (Quiet rage.) Sitting on a pile of mouldy kittywake
               pelts. No label. No display case. No nothing! Just
               an unopened crate…in a huge basement full of
               unopened crates.

               (DICKASON is stunned.)

DICKASON: All for nothing, sir? None of it mattered?

PRIESTLEY: I'm afraid not.

               *(Pause. DICKASON brims up. PRIESTLEY is
               shocked by the suddenness of his reaction.)*

DICKASON: I'm sorry, sir. Entirely inappropriate.

PRIESTLEY: I didn't mean to…

               *(DICKASON retrieves the chronometer from his
               pocket, holds it out to PRIESTLEY.)*

DICKASON: You keep this, Sir Raymond. I've no need of it.

PRIESTLEY: *(Tender.)* Come with me. There's something I want
               to show you.

DICKASON: *(Following him off.)* What did we do, sir? What did
               we really do?

PRIESTLEY: Shh.

               *(Light cross-fade to: CAMPBELL, ABBOTT,
               LEVICK and BROWNING lie in a row.
               CAMPBELL sketches in his journal.)*

LEVICK: Nature, in the form of man, begins to recognize
               itself. That's what we're doing here in the South,
               Lieutenant. We are all artists, of a kind. We are
               giving nature back to herself. Every man-Jack of us.

CAMPBELL: *(Not convinced.)* Noble thought, Mother.

LEVICK: Your pencil studies.

CAMPBELL: I'm merely filling time.

LEVICK: Nonsense. You have a fine eye for landscape and the nuance of natural light. You are bringing new geography into the human imagination.

CAMPBELL: It's a distraction, Dr. Levick. Nothing more.

LEVICK: Surely not.

CAMPBELL: We focus on the outside to avoid the whirlwind within.

            (Pause.)

LEVICK: I see that in you.

CAMPBELL: Oh?

LEVICK: A solitary soul. Takes one to know one.

CAMPBELL: The reserve of a lifetime is not easily broken.

LEVICK: Of course not. It's been built up to protect the sensitive bits. Which we all have...

            (Pause.)

            Men are born incomplete. That's my view.

CAMPBELL: Oh?

LEVICK: They spend their lives searching for the missing part. The feminine.

CAMPBELL: Hm.

LEVICK: This German chap has some interesting theories on the subject. The book should be out in English by the time we return home.

            (ABBOTT fights clear of his bag, coughing and sputtering.)

ABBOTT: Get off! Get off!

LEVICK: Are you alright?

ABBOTT: Nightmare. The whole world pressing in on me face. No air to breathe. Nowhere to go.

LEVICK: There, there.

ABBOTT: There is something wrong with the air in here.

CAMPBELL: Smitch from the cooker. Nothing to be done, unfortunately.

BROWNING: I could design a chimney.

LEVICK: *(To CAMPBELL.)* We might want to reconsider…

CAMPBELL: Out of the question. I've been watching that crack. It's getting bigger.

LEVICK: Throbbing? *(ABBOTT nods.)* Good. That means the blood supply is secure.

             (ABBOTT studies his hand.)

ABBOTT: Gentlemen, it is official. Part of me has died.

LEVICK: I'm going to save your hand.

ABBOTT: Don't tell me a story.

CAMPBELL: Mind over matter.

LEVICK: As long as there is a blood supply—

ABBOTT: I don't need to hear a fucking story, Mother! This black moves up my arm! That is the story!

CAMPBELL: You are feeling sorry for yourself! Go to sleep! That is an order!

             (ABBOTT disappears into his bag. Long pause. CAMPBELL draws in his journal.)

             Did you just say something?

LEVICK: No sir.

CAMPBELL: I heard you say: Be gentle with him.

LEVICK: I didn't say a word, sir.

CAMPBELL: I must be tired. Do you ever hear voices when you're tired?

LEVICK: Not as a rule.

               (Pause. CAMPBELL draws.)

               Did you find your pencil?

CAMPBELL: No. I am greatly disturbed by it. I leave the thing securely fastened to the spine of my journal. There's no possibility of it going missing. May I borrow yours?

               This one is a number ten.

               (LEVICK offers his pencil. CAMPBELL sketches in his journal.)

LEVICK: Abbott means no harm.

CAMPBELL: Dr. Levick, your ability to form relationships across social boundaries is nothing short of miraculous. You're rather an enigma to me, sir. You are both fore and aft.

LEVICK: It is my fate to have confidential chats with people who have confidences to bestow. It's always been that way for me. My mother's influence, I should think.

CAMPBELL: Intimacy must be a terrifying burden.

LEVICK: Why?

CAMPBELL: Where does it end? Can there be no secrets? Can nothing remain hidden?

LEVICK: Everything is hidden. That is the whole problem.

CAMPBELL: Less said, soonest mended. That was the watchword of my upbringing.

LEVICK: I think that's a very old-fashioned view. The modern age demands a higher level of honesty from us.

CAMPBELL: I despise the modern age.

LEVICK: No avoiding it.

CAMPBELL: Unless you come to a place like this.

LEVICK: No! *(Tapping head.)* It's all in here, you see, in the products of our thinking. A wall to wall intellectual revolution.

As much as anything that's what has carried us here on this pilgrimage. The South Pole is an idea. A place that is no place. The final nothing.

CAMPBELL: I'm afraid I don't see it.

(CAMPBELL feigns interest in his journal.)

LEVICK: A voyage to zero. The entire world reduced to the inside of this…this skull.

CAMPBELL: Someone has been in my journal.

LEVICK: Oh?

CAMPBELL: Fingerprints, smudges. These markings here.

(He holds up a grubby page for the doctor's inspection, moving it away before he has a chance to read.)

LEVICK: Are you sure?

CAMPBELL: We'll find out soon enough.

(Pause. LEVICK watches CAMPBELL obsess.)

LEVICK: Lieutenant Campbell, at the beginning of this expedition you asked that I advise you of any signs of mental slippage in the group. You wanted it nipped in the bud.

CAMPBELL: Are you questioning my command, Dr. Levick?

LEVICK: Certainly not. We are all near the breaking point. I think you're holding up rather well. *(Pause.)* I was more worried about myself.

CAMPBELL: Feeling a bit rocky?

LEVICK: I am thinking so much. Perhaps too much. A great noise in my head. It's like the wind out there. It just keeps blowing and I can't seem to stop it. I move backwards and forwards in time, sifting great mountains of detail. This connects to that and, aha,

I have another Conclusion which I file under 'C'
right next to Contradiction and the Contradiction
prevents my Conclusion from being conclusive
and, in the next instant, I'm with my mother in
Wiltshire tending her peonies and I feel this aston-
ishing surge of...of longing for something that is
gone...never to return...and I realize that when my
mind thinks...it hides...and that I shall never in my
life find peace or happiness... *(Pause.)* My life is a
tomb. I dare not speak its secrets.

CAMPBELL: Less said, soonest mended, Dr. Levick.

LEVICK: I don't know what I'm telling you. I am simply
             asking that you monitor my behaviour and tell me
             to take my rest when I need it. If one came unstrung
             in this setting it would have a terrible effect on the
             well-being of the party as a whole.

             (Pause.)

CAMPBELL: Yes. Rather cramped quarters for a full-on, raving
             lunacy.

             (They laugh. A crazed moment. A pause.)

LEVICK: I fear for my soul. Lead us. Save us. O dear God...

             (LEVICK weeps.)

CAMPBELL: Say the Lord's Prayer with me.

LEVICK: No. It doesn't help now.

CAMPBELL: *(Singing.)* "The Lord is my shepherd—"

LEVICK: NO! I'm sorry. I must sleep.

             (Pause. LEVICK settles into his bag.)

CAMPBELL: You would tell me if there was cause for real
             alarm?

LEVICK: Of course, sir. Immediately.

CAMPBELL: On both sides, I mean. With me as well as with
             you...

LEVICK: I think that's what I'm doing, sir. We must sleep.

               (Long pause. CAMPBELL leafs through his journal.)

CAMPBELL: There. Again. Your voice. What are you thinking?

LEVICK: My mind is filling the world, sir.

               (Pause.)

CAMPBELL: I believe you.

               (LEVICK and CAMPBELL settle into their bags.

               Light shift: to favour the Cambridge drawing room, still dimmed. The air is warm and reddish gold with firelight.

               DICKASON sits in the chair, forlorn.)

DICKASON: I don't know what to believe now, sir.

PRIESTLEY: *(Off.)* Close your eyes and keep them closed.

               (PRIESTLEY appears and stands before DICKASON, puts a grubby canvas sack in his hands.)

DICKASON: What is it, sir?

PRIESTLEY: A world.

               (DICKASON handles the bag.)

               A world like no other…

DICKASON: I don't follow, sir.

PRIESTLEY: Open your eyes.

DICKASON: *(Stunned.)* Is this really it?

PRIESTLEY: One falls back on the testimony of things, Dickie. *(Whisper.)* The glacier burnished silver. The stars, steel points.

DICKASON: The crunch of the snow underfoot…

               (Pause.)

PRIESTLEY: *(Fear and wonder.)* I have grown to be so alone. I stay in these rooms for weeks.

DICKASON: *(His own version.)* I sit by the window, smoke my pipe. *(Pause.)* Gone South.

PRIESTLEY: Talk to me. Take me back there.

DICKASON: Oh that I could...

PRIESTLEY: The worst of it. That's what I need to understand.

DICKASON: Abbott. On his way to the madhouse.

        (Sound: moan of air raid siren.)

        May I open it, Mr. Nipcheese?

PRIESTLEY: All clear.

        (DICKASON has his hand in the bag. He doesn't need to withdraw it. He closes his eyes.)

DICKASON: Muscatel. Muscatel. Muscatel.

        (Sound: the air raid siren becomes the wind.

        Light shift: We are back on the ice cap in a roaring storm. DICKASON holds the bag aloft.)

DICKASON: Mr. Priestley! The day bag! I found the missing day bag!

        (Light: snap to black.

        Sound: coughing, hacking and wheezing.)

CAMPBELL: *(Off.)* LIGHTS! Where are the lights!

ABBOTT: *(Off.)* I can't breathe!

LEVICK: *(Off.)* We're suffocating!

BROWNING: *(Off.)* Help!

CAMPBELL: *(Off.)* Light! Bring me some light!

PRIESTLEY: *(Off.)* The lamps went out! You're asphyxiating!

DICKASON: *(Off.)* The tunnel! Quickly!

(Light shift: to low levels, as the men pile out onto the ice, coughing and wheezing on their hands and knees.

DICKASON and PRIESTLEY are in better shape, ministering to the rest.)

We could smell the fumes out here.

PRIESTLEY: From the cooker.

LEVICK: Another minute and we'd have been goners.

CAMPBELL: A chimney. Browning you must set about designing a chimney.

BROWNING: Yes sir. *(To ABBOTT.)* Could you warm me?

LEVICK: *(To CAMPBELL.)* Back from the dead.

              (We hold the epic tableau.

              Light: the pop of a flashbulb.)

DICKASON: Look!

              (All look skyward.

              Light: Aurora Australis. Curtains of mauve light.)

BROWNING: The aurora.

              (Music under: Meredith Monk.)

DICKASON: *(Whisper.)* The roaring loom…

LEVICK: Lovely, Mr. Dickason.

DICKASON: I understand the cut of it now, sir. The awe…

              (DICKASON holds out the canvas sack to CAMPBELL.)

PRIESTLEY: He found the missing day bag, sir.

LEVICK: *(To CAMPBELL.)* We are lucky men. *(Pause.)* Lead us. Save us.

CAMPBELL: We will feast tonight. We will celebrate Midwinter's Eve.

LEVICK: We've got a month yet, sir.

CAMPBELL: I hereby erase that month and set the calendar forward. I command it!

                (Big cheer from the men.)

                And following our feast we shall have a great debate, and following that a spellbinding lecture
                from Dr. Levick and following that a hymn sing so
                grand that it will shake the very walls of Heaven!
                Mr. Nipcheese, uncrate extra rations from the
                sledge. Four biscuits! Twelve lumps of sugar!
                Twenty muscatels! Four sticks of chocolate! Sweet
                thick cocoa! Wincarnis!

                (Huge cheer at the mention of alcohol.)

                Give thanks! We are back from the dead! It is Midwinter's Eve! We are on our way to the light!

LEVICK: The worst is over?

PRIESTLEY: Homeward bound!

BROWNING: *(Singing.)* So haul along the pier my boys.

ALL: *(Singing.)* So haul along the pier my boys.

BROWNING: *(Singing.)* And never mind the storm!

ALL: And never mind the storm! / For when our money
                all is spent / We'll go and work for more / And to
                those who will not merry merry be / We'll never
                share our joy / Sing, Sing, The boys in blue have
                won the victory.

                (They light candles in the cave.)

ALL: And if ever I return again / And if ever I return
                again / And if ever I return again / I'll make you
                my bride.

                *(A festive air achieved with the arrangement of extra candles and seal oil lamps. The men are sitting
                with enormous stacks of food in their laps.)*

CAMPBELL: The scripture reading is from the Book of Job, verse
                38, 29–30.

Out of whose womb came the ice? And the hoary frost of Heaven, who hath conceived it? The waters are hid as with a stone, and the face of the deep is frozen.

> (*ABBOTT looks up. His face is terrifying.*)

ALL: (*Except ABBOTT.*) Amen.

> (*ABBOTT tips back his seal head and sucks juices.*)

CAMPBELL: Gentlemen, it's two and a half years since we left the dock in London.

LEVICK: Appropriate moment for some toasting, I should think.

PRIESTLEY: Everyone got their wincarnis?

CAMPBELL: To the King.

PRIESTLEY: To those at home. Wives and sweethearts.

LEVICK: May they never meet.

> (*Laughter.*)

DICKASON: To Commander Scott and his triumph at the Pole.

BROWNING: To Abbott. Killer of seals.

CAMPBELL: Mr. Abbott?

> (*ABBOTT is busy digging at his seal head.*)

ABBOTT: I think you've about covered it.

LEVICK: You must toast with us, Tiny. Tradition demands it.

ABBOTT: (*Raising his skull to CAMPBELL.*) To the Pharaoh. Long may he reign.

> (*They raise cups.*)

I was being facetious.

> (*BROWNING and DICKASON laugh. ABBOTT drains his wincarnis.*)

ABBOTT: *(cont'd)* That's a punch in the face.

                   (CAMPBELL refills ABBOTT's cup.)

CAMPBELL: You like your drink, Tiny. We knew that.

ABBOTT: *(Toasting them.)* Raise steam in all boilers!

CAMPBELL: As of this moment, we're coasting home with the
                   wind at our backs.

                   (Cheer.)

DICKASON: I'm going to chisel this date into the rock.

CAMPBELL: Splendid.

BROWNING: We've outdone the bloody Egyptians, we have.

                   *(ABBOTT plays the nose flute and mimes his cobra
                   hand. Pointing his blackened finger at the others one
                   by one.)*

ABBOTT: *(To LEVICK.)* The fickle finger of death. Who goes
                   first? Who goes last?

                   (LEVICK laughs uproarously.)

LEVICK: You have powerful eyes. Did anyone ever tell you
                   that?

CAMPBELL: *(Overriding.)* Fine idea, Dickie. Chisel us into the
                   rock. We must mark our passing.

                   *(ABBOTT pours himself another drink. Swigs from
                   the bottle.)*

LEVICK: *(Indicating the cave.)* This is the whole world. You
                   know that, don't you?

BROWNING: Well, for the time being at least.

LEVICK: No, really. I—I was thinking about it last night. The
                   six of us, inside this...this skull, we have stopped
                   time. All that has been. All that will be. The light
                   before, the light after...the darkness between.
                   Nothing. The final zero.

BROWNING: As you say, sir.

LEVICK: The fundus. The fundament. The firmament. F. G
               follows F. And G is for…

               *(ABBOTT points his finger at the crack. Makes his
               sizzling sound. LEVICK looks to CAMPBELL.
               Smiles.)*

               I'm afraid I've lost my train of thought.

ABBOTT: Lucky boy. Here's to you.

CAMPBELL: I should like each man to affix his fingerprints to a
               sheet in my journal and sign it. We shall secure the
               pages in a tea cannister and leave them here for
               posterity.

PRIESTLEY: First rate, Lieutenant.

LEVICK: In Sumeria they left handprints on the cave walls. I
               have seen them.

               *(CAMPBELL opens his journal to a fresh page.
               ABBOTT points at the ceiling and makes his
               sizzling sound.)*

CAMPBELL: You'll need no ink pad.

BROWNING: Such a load of food.

DICKASON: And when he adds in his trove of muscatels.

               *(LEVICK brings forward his stash. Funny motor-
               cycle noise.)*

BROWNING: Da-ding, da-ding, the door to the South Pole is al-
               ways open. My sugars.

               (BROWNING unwraps his stash of sugars.)

ABBOTT: *(To LEVICK.)* Jam them in. *(Whisper.)* Do it for me.

LEVICK: *(Handing them to ABBOTT.)* Take what you need
               and pass the rest on.

               (A moment of stunned silence.)

ABBOTT: How many do I take?

LEVICK: There are ninety-six.

BROWNING: That's sixteen each.

ABBOTT: *(To BROWNING.)* I'll trade you ten muscatels for two sugars.

              (Pause. BROWNING hands his sugars to LEVICK.)

BROWNING: Take what you need, pass them on.

PRIESTLEY: Has there ever been a better ship's company?

LEVICK: Hear, hear! The Great Debate! *(To the men.)* Alright over there on the mess deck, have you got a worthy subject for us?

              (ABBOTT drinks deep, hands CAMPBELL his pencil.)

ABBOTT: Found your pencil.

CAMPBELL: Where?

ABBOTT: Under Dickie's bag.

              (DICKASON says nothing. ABBOTT refills his cup.)

LEVICK: We're losing ground here! The debate!

              (The journal returns to CAMPBELL's hands. He sets about comparing thumbprints with other markings in the filthy pages.)

ABBOTT: I got a fucking topic.

BROWNING: It's got to begin with the word 'resolved'.

ABBOTT: Fuck 'resolved', I say that every man in England should be allowed to shoot rabbits on any man's land. Who is with me?

PRIESTLEY: Wait a minute, Tiny. That's not how a debate works.

LEVICK: We discuss it. People take opposite sides. The pros and the cons.

ABBOTT: Fine, let's discuss it. I'll tell you a little story.

There's a man in Cornwall who owns twenty thousand acres. The Duke of something-or-other.

CAMPBELL: The Earl of Carlyle. I know the man. Go on.

ABBOTT: When I was a lad me father was out of work a good deal and we was often hungry. What should stop me, a hungry young lad, from climbing a fence to fetch food for his starving family? This Duke was never even on the premises.

PRIESTLEY: You have a hazy understanding of property law, Tiny.

ABBOTT: I'll tell you where it goes if we leave things as they are. Millions upon millions of rabbits behind fences, all of them belonging to some lucky sperm who happened to find his way between the right pair of legs.

BROWNING: Sounds like the Royal Family.

ABBOTT: Dead on.

(BROWNING and ABBOTT roar with laughter.)

CAMPBELL: The monarchy is out-of-bounds. We are here in His Majesty's service.

PRIESTLEY: Where do *you* draw the line, Abbott? If Carlyle lets you shoot rabbits on his land is that enough?

ABBOTT: Nothing is enough. Let's fucking vote.

PRIESTLEY: You are against the rule of law.

ABBOTT: More and more in the hands of the few? If that's what you call the rule of law then I'm against it.

CAMPBELL: I suppose it all depends on the values one receives in the home.

ABBOTT: Undoubtedly. *(Pause.)* I grew up in an Egyptian tomb.

(LEVICK chuckles. ABBOTT swigs from the bottle.)

LEVICK: Tell us more!

ABBOTT: I watched my father get murdered. Right outside
               the back door.

               (Stunned silence.)

               He was a poor twisted soul and the man that done
               him in was worse yet. Family fight, you see. Both
               dead drunk at the time. Out of work. Nothing to
               eat. And all of a sudden there's my father spinning
               around on the ground with his throat slit. *(Pause.)*
               Little me standing over him. My mother screaming
               from the kitchen door. Blood everywhere. *(Pause.)*
               There. Now you know something. *(Swigs from
               bottle.)* Drink of this in memory of me.

               *(He passes the bottle to LEVICK. LEVICK hesi-
               tates, drinks deeply.*

               *CAMPBELL flips back and forth between pages in
               his journal. He has found a match. An uncomfort-
               able pause.)*

LEVICK: If I could chime in with an adjacent thought here, I
               often think what a huge responsibility we who
               employ servants incur by doing so.

               (ABBOTT snorts a laugh.)

CAMPBELL: Dickason, were you reading my journal?

DICKASON: No sir.

CAMPBELL: Are you sure?

DICKASON: Yes sir.

               (ABBOTT relishes their exchange.)

LEVICK: Our servants have given their lives to save time for
               the lucky few and, one by one, we, the lucky few,
               will be brought face to face with them and asked
               what we have done with our lives and the time
               they gave us to make the world a better place.

CAMPBELL: This is your thumbprint.

DICKASON: No sir.

ABBOTT: Excuse me, Mother. Nothing the man with all the rabbits is doing is making the world a better place. That's a complete fantasy.

CAMPBELL: A sneak.

DICKASON: No.

LEVICK: Take my own case, I'm a man with a few rabbits, I can point to my Emperor Penguin eggs and say that in my own small way—

ABBOTT: Hauling those fucking penguin eggs back to England does not make the world a better place!

PRIESTLEY: He is adding to the store of the world's knowledge!

ABBOTT: Rubbish!

CAMPBELL: A sneak!

PRIESTLEY: Human progress is not rubbish!

CAMPBELL: This is your thumbprint, Dickason!

LEVICK: I'm afraid we're getting off-topic here.

CAMPBELL: I think you need a taste of the wind, my boy. OUT! MOVE!

            (ABBOTT moves to block CAMPBELL's eye line and protect DICKASON.)

ABBOTT: More and more falling into the hands of the few. My prediction? There will be a great cleansing of the system and it will come sooner than you lot think!

            (ABBOTT is looking at his dead finger. He points it at CAMPBELL.)

            BLOOD WILL RUN IN THE STREETS!

LEVICK: The minnows, Tiny. Remember the minnows.

ABBOTT: Don't bite the hand that feeds us? Mind over matter?

(ABBOTT puts his black finger in his mouth. Bites down on it. Harder and harder. An audible crunch.)

LEVICK: Good Lord.

(LEVICK and PRIESTLEY move to minister to ABBOTT. ABBOTT's face bulges. He makes a terrible sizzling sound. He's up on his haunches now. Pure animal aggression. He leans into PRIESTLEY.)

ABBOTT: *(Hiss.)* No man touches me.

(PRIESTLEY looks into the eye of the storm. The soul with the lizard's tail.)

BROWNING: *(Horror.)* Let's fucking vote.

LEVICK: Resolved that Parliament should enact a new law that allows every man in England to hunt rabbits on any man's land. All in favour?

(ABBOTT shoots his hand up high. He looks to BROWNING. After a pause, BROWNING raises his hand. They look to DICKASON to join their ranks. DICKASON hesitates, looks to CAMPBELL.)

CAMPBELL: Dear Dickie. What will become of you when all the rabbits are gone?

(LEVICK raises his hand, looks to DICKASON. Pause. DICKASON raises his hand, tentative, then with growing resolve.)

PRIESTLEY: We seem to be outnumbered here.

CAMPBELL: *(Crazed.)* Lower the portcullis! Prepare the vats of molten lead! All hands on deck for a flogging! Set the topsail! Raise steam!

(Light shift: to isolate CAMPBELL in a single. He lifts men into the rigging with tiny tweezers.)

You sail with Drake, Raleigh and Cook! Tiny faces under a magnifying glass. *(To LEVICK.)* Make my own brushes, you see. The emblem on the sleeve.

(To ABBOTT.) Now there's a tight corner. *(To LEVICK.)* Three or four strands of Russian sable does the trick.

> *(He applies tiny brush strokes to the palm of his hand.)*

(Looking up.) Is this my face? Is that what I paint? My own face? Over and over and over again.

> *(Light shift: the spot tightens further around CAMPBELL.)*

The final emptiness. *(Whisper.)* Priests with jackal heads move in the shadows...the rustle of their garments...surely there will be some ceremony. *(Pause.)* They put long hooks up the nostril and pull out the brain. The last boundary is down. The wind rises. The wind! THE WIND!

> *(Sound: massive wind burst.*
>
> *Light: snap to black.*
>
> *Light shift: to playing levels.*
>
> *CAMPBELL groans in his bag. He is hidden from view.)*

BROWNING: *(Whisper, to LEVICK.)* Is he alright?

LEVICK: He needs his rest.

CAMPBELL: *(Weak.)* I shall be just fine.

> *(CAMPBELL rolls onto his stomach. A child with a broken heart.)*

LEVICK: Sleep, sir. It will help you regain yourself.

CAMPBELL: I need no rest. I need your voice, Mother. I think we all need to hear the sound of your voice.

PRIESTLEY: A fire to warm the hands.

LEVICK: Topic?

CAMPBELL: Human progress in the Modern Age.

LEVICK: Large subject. Where to begin? The compass. The cathedral. The chronometer. *(Taps his forehead.)* All up here. A question of getting things in the proper order. That is always the problem. *(To DICKASON.)* Name a letter.

DICKASON: D.

LEVICK: Fine. Let us begin with the letter D. D is for... Darwin. Charles Darwin. 1809–1882. Naturalist of great patience and zeal. Buried in Westminster Abbey beside Sir Isaac Newton. Theory of natural selection. Egg cracks open. Aha!

               Laws governing the emergence of new life forms! A glimpse of Nature's plan! Orthodoxy of the day. Unseen Deity. Evolution preordained, therefore inherently progressive. Rubbish! The first idol Darwin toppled was God.

PRIESTLEY: Given a watch we infer a watchmaker.

LEVICK: And we are wrong! *(Tender, to DICKASON.)* Keeping up, Dickie?

DICKASON: Not entirely.

CAMPBELL: *(Weak protest.)* Dr. Levick—

LEVICK: We are trying to learn something here about the animal ancestry of man! Let me give you an example. Every large-brained mammal harbours in its gut species of parasites so morphologically 'degenerate' that they are little more than bags of reproductive tissue. According to Darwin it is impossible to say whether the host or the parasite is 'better' or any surer of evolutionary persistence. The life forms exist alongside each other as absolute equals. That is man's proper place in the history of Nature!

DICKASON: Are you saying that I'm no better than the parasite in Browning's gut?

LEVICK: That is exactly what I am saying!

ABBOTT: YES! YES! YES!

LEVICK: There is NO PLAN! Every living thing we see in nature is a by-product of the struggle for existence between individuals. Nothing more.

CAMPBELL: I'm afraid I can't agree.

LEVICK: Look at the Greeley expedition!

CAMPBELL: Dr. Levick.

LEVICK: Stranded as we are the men turned to cannibalism. Ellison, the leader, had lost both his hands and feet to frostbite. He could do nothing to stop it.

(ABBOTT growls with pleasure.)

CAMPBELL: Dr. Levick!

LEVICK: There was a well-worn trail from cave to grave-yard! They never spoke of it!

ABBOTT: Of course not! Too polite!

CAMPBELL: Dr. Levick, I must ask that—

(CAMPBELL sits up. Regaining himself.)

LEVICK: Those who were strong enough to take the path to survival simply took it, and thereby—

CAMPBELL: DR. LEVICK! I don't think it's appropriate that we draw conclusions based on the experience of men who behaved like rats in a trap.

LEVICK: Rats in a trap. Exactly so.

Welcome to the Modern Age.

(Pause.)

BROWNING: No God watches over us?

LEVICK: I'm sorry...I...

(Pause. BROWNING begins to hum/sing "Peril on the Sea".)

PRIESTLEY: Are you alright, sir?

LEVICK: For some unaccountable reason I seem to be weeping. You must excuse me...

CAMPBELL: Oh dear.

ABBOTT: *(To BROWNING.)* Your tea shop is called 'The South Pole'.

LEVICK: My thinking.*(To CAMPBELL.)* Can you hear it? I can hear it. It is so loud.

ABBOTT: *(To BROWNING.)* You sit by the fire and tell your tall tales.

LEVICK: One day on the ice I was busy with my watercolours and an Emperor Penguin came right up to stand before me. I stared into his golden eye...and I saw...my thinking...

ABBOTT: *(To BROWNING.)* Da-ding, da-ding. The missus serving cream teas. All very tidy.

               (BROWNING continues to hum/sing the hymn.)

PRIESTLEY: Your thinking, doctor?

LEVICK: It has come unstuck. Everything. I have been holding on to so much for so long. I am no longer strong enough. I cannot hold this world in my mind. That is not my job! It must all fall free. All the shelves emptying out into a gigantic pile on the floor. The whirling, screaming chaos of it!

               (CAMPBELL puts his arms around LEVICK.)

CAMPBELL: Dr. Levick—

LEVICK: *(Breaking free.)* Smash! Smash! The idols are falling! I have seen paintings in Paris where the face is splayed like a fern frond pressed flat in a book! Books no longer have plots! Plays are about nothing! Portraits don't look like people! Goods and services race around at breakneck speed. We fly! We communicate across oceans! What does it mean? Are we still on 'D'? Disorientation. Dissolution. Despair.

CAMPBELL: *(Comforting him.)* There, there. We shall bring Mother back around. We shall do it together.

(Pause.)

LEVICK: The world falls like a great chandelier.

(Pause.)

That is the end of my lecture.

CAMPBELL: *(Upbeat.)* Fine then. The idols have all been toppled. The world has come crashing down around us. Campbell chooses the letter C. C is for Contradiction. Give us the other side now, human progress.

(Pause.)

LEVICK: The great wheel turns, inch by inch. We take our place alongside the animals and begin again. This cave is the childhood of the world. A Golden Age where we live in perfect harmony with nature. A profound, unspoken understanding. There is no distinction between us and the wild things. The lion stalks near the fire and I smell him. The penguin stands before me and...there is no thinking...I swim in his golden eye.

CAMPBELL: Mr. Priestley, brew up some tea for Dr. Levick's return. Make yourself busy, Dickie, chisel us into the rock.

(PRIESTLEY and DICKASON move off.)

ABBOTT: Are we in the future?

LEVICK: No. It is twenty-five thousand years ago.

PREISTLY: The end of the last Ice Age.

LEVICK: We were hunters then. We lived entirely in the present. Our five senses were much more finely tuned. We stalked by smell in the night.

BROWNING: What did we eat in this Golden Age?

LEVICK: Giant Sloth. Mastodon. Cave Bear.

CAMPBELL: One presumes this is before language.

LEVICK: Before memory...

> *(Pause. DICKASON appears in the vanishing point and hits rock with chisel and mallet.)*

BROWNING: The Modern Age.

ABBOTT: An ice cave.

> *(PRIESTLEY sits in his chair.)*

PRIESTLEY: Inexpressible Island.

LEVICK: Nature has re-entered us. *(To CAMPBELL.)* Perhaps that is what we are experiencing. *(Pause.)* The penetrating member of Nature.

BROWNING: I feel it at night, a scraping in my chest.

ABBOTT: *(Tender.)* Be not afraid. I will save you.

CAMPBELL: We will survive. I command it.

BROWNING: *(To CAMPBELL.)* Thank you.*(To ABBOTT.)* Thank you.

CAMPBELL: Everyone out for a freshener! Come on, Tiny! Show us what you're made of.

DICKASON: You heard the Lieutenant, Mr. Nipcheese! You're a Blue Jacket now! Step lively!

> *(A look between DICKASON and PRIESTLEY. The joy of belonging.*
>
> *Lights fade. Everyone moves in slow motion.*
>
> *One candle remains lit beside PRIESTLEY.)*

PRIESTLEY: Campbell!

CAMPBELL: *(Echoing.)* Campbell, Campbell, Campbell.

> *(CAMPBELL appears in a crouch.)*

PRIESTLEY: Levick!

LEVICK: *(Echoing.)* Levick, Levick, Levick.

(LEVICK positions himself in front of CAMPBELL, slightly more erect.)

PRIESTLEY: Dickason!

DICKASON: *(Echoing.)* Dickason, Dickason, Dickason.

(DICKASON takes a position in front of LEVICK, slightly more erect.)

PRIESTLEY: Browning!

BROWNING: *(Echoing.)* Browning, Browning, Browning.

(BROWNING moves to take a semi-upright stance in front of DICKASON.)

PRIESTLEY: Abbott.

ABBOTT: Abbott!

(ABBOTT moves into place. Fully erect. The New Man emerging from the chaos of the cave. He carries BROWNING on his back.

PRIESTLEY stands and moves down the line of men.)

PRIESTLEY: A hard night full of absent friends. Clear. A blue sky so deep that it looks black. The stars, steel points. The glacier burnished silver. A single undulating arch of brilliant light, a tail of flaming gold, crossing the sky like the curved blade of a scimitar. Who is there to see? To listen? To remember?

(Sound: wind.)

The wind rises. Footprints vanish in the drift.

(PRIESTLEY takes his position in the evolutionary line.)

The sun turns and comes back to us tonight.

(To black.

*Light effect: a pulse of golden light from the hearth.
The light builds, boils up into a pillar of fire.*

Snap to black.

Music up: Meredith Monk.

First curtain: "I Vow to Thee My Country".

The End.)

Acknowledgements

Above all, I would like to thank Richard Rose, my first and best reader. Special thanks also to Monte Alford, who told me the story in a storm-bound tent on a mountain in the Yukon and to the Scott Polar Research Institute in Cambridge which provided access to a treasure trove of research materials.

I would also like to thank the following: Patsy Aldana, Margaret Atwood, George D. Butterfield, Suzette Couture, Jill Fraser, Duncan Ollerenshaw, Michael Ondaatje, Rick Roberts, Carl and Shirley Roth, Dr. Peter Steele, Dr. Ross Woodman and Ronald Wright.

I am indebted to the following authors and books: Raymond E. Priestly, *Scott's Northern Party*; Victor Campbell, *The Wicked Mate*; Jan Morris, *Pax Britannica*; Apsley Cherry-Garrard, *The Worst Journey in the World*; Francis Spufford, *I May Be Some Time: Ice and the English Imagination*; A.J. Spencer, *Death in Ancient Egypt*; Benjamin Farrington and Stephen Jay Gould, *What Darwin Really Said*; Captain John Wells, *The Royal Navy: An Illustrated Social History*; Elspeth Huxley, *Scott of the Antarctic*; Beryl Bainbridge, *The Birthday Boys*; and Roland Huntford, *Shackelton*.